3/94

UNIVERSITY OF
WOLVERHAMPT~

HEAL HAL RNING

EXPERIMENTAL
RESEARCH 2

Start date

Target completion date

Tutor for this topic

Contact number

WITHDRAWN

USING THIS WORKBOOK

The workbook is divided into 'Sessions', covering specific subjects.

In the introduction to each learning pack there is a learner profile to help you assess your current knowledge of the subjects covered in each session.

Each session has clear learning objectives. They indicate what you will be able to achieve or learn by completing that session.

Each session has a summary to remind you of the key points of the subjects covered.

Each session contains text, diagrams and learning activities that relate to the stated objectives.

It is important to complete each activity, making your own notes and writing in answers in the space provided. **Remember this is your own workbook—you are allowed to write on it**.

Now try an example activity.

ACTIVITY

This activity shows you what happens when cells work without oxygen. This really is a physical activity, so please only try it if you are fully fit.

First, raise one arm straight up in the air above your head, and let the other hand rest by your side. Clench both fists tightly, and then open out your fingers wide. Repeat this at the rate of once or twice a second. Try to keep clenching both fists at the same rate. Keep going for about five minutes, and record what you observe.

Stop and rest for a minute. Then try again, with the opposite arm raised this time. Again, record your observations.

Suggested timings are given for each activity. These are only a guide. You may like to note how long it took you to complete this activity, as it may help in planning the time needed for working through the sessions.

Time taken on activity

Time management is important. While we recognise that people learn at different speeds, this pack is designed to take 35 study hours (your tutor will also advise you). You should allocate time during each week for study.

Take some time now to identify likely periods that you can set aside for study during the week.

	Mon	Tues	Wed	Thurs	Fri	Sat	Sun
am							
pm							
eve							

At the end of the learning pack, there is a learning review to help you assess whether you have achieved the learning objectives.

HEALTHCARE ACTIVE LEARNING

HAL

EXPERIMENTAL RESEARCH 2

CONDUCTING AND REPORTING EXPERIMENTAL RESEARCH

Stephanie Keeble BA (Hons) Psychology

Senior Lecturer, University of West of England at Bristol

THE OPEN LEARNING FOUNDATION

CHURCHILL LIVINGSTONE

EDINBURGH LONDON MADRID MELBOURNE NEW YORK AND TOKYO 1995

CHURCHILL LIVINGSTONE
Medical Division of Longman Group UK Limited

Distributed in the United States of America by Churchill
Livingstone Inc., 650 Avenue of the Americas, New York,
N.Y. 10011, and by associated companies, branches and
representatives throughout the world.

First published 1995

ISBN 0 443 05271 9

British Library of Cataloguing in Publication Data
A catalogue record for this book is available from the
British Library.

Library of Congress Cataloging in Publication Data
A catalogue record for this book is available from the
Library of Congress

Printed and bound by Bell and Bain Ltd., Glasgow

For The Open Learning Foundation

Director of Programmes: Leslie Mapp
Series Editor: Robert Adams
Programmes Manager: Kathleen Farren
Production Manager: Steve Moulds

For Churchill Livingstone

Director (NAH): Peter Shepherd
Project Development Editor: Mairi McCubbin
Project Manager: Valerie Burgess
Design Direction: Judith Wright
Pre-press Project Manager: Neil Dickson
Pre-press Desktop Operator: Kate Walshaw
Sales Promotion Executive: Hilary Brown

CONTENTS

OPEN LEARNING
FOUNDATION
TEAM MEMBERS

Writer: Stephanie Keeble
Senior Lecturer, University of West of England at Bristol

Editor: Diane West
Open Learning Editor

Reviewers: Mike Hyland
Reader in Health Psychology, University of Plymouth

Professor Norma Reid
Head of Department and Professor of Health Sciences,
Chair of Faculty of Social, Biological and Health Science,
Coventry University

Series Editor: Robert Adams
OLF Programme Head,
Social Work and Health and Nursing,
University of Humberside

THE OPEN LEARNING FOUNDATION

Higher education has grown considerably in recent years. As well as catering for more students, universities are facing the challenge of providing for an increasingly diverse student population. Students have a wider range of backgrounds and previous educational qualifications. There are greater numbers of mature students. There is a greater need for part-time courses and continuing education and professional development programmes.

The Open Learning Foundation helps over 20 member institutions meet this growing and diverse demand – through the production of high-quality teaching and learning materials, within a strategy of creating a framework for more flexible learning. It offers member institutions the capability to increase their range of teaching options and to cover subjects in greater breadth and depth.

It does not enrol its own students. Rather, The Open Learning Foundation, by developing and promoting the greater use of open and distance learning, enables universities and others in higher education to make study more accessible and cost-effective for individual students and for business through offering more choice and more flexible courses.

Formed in 1990, the Foundation's policy objectives are to:

- improve the quality of higher education and training

- increase the quantity of higher education and training

- raise the efficiency of higher education and training delivery.

In working to meet these objectives, The Open Learning Foundation develops new teaching and learning materials, encourages and facilitates more and better staff development, and promotes greater responsiveness to change within higher education institutions. The Foundation works in partnership with its members and other higher education bodies to develop new approaches to teaching and learning.

In developing new teaching and learning materials, the Foundation has:

- a track record of offering customers a swift and flexible response

- a national network of members able to provide local support and guidance

- the ability to draw on significant national expertise in producing and delivering open learning

- complete freedom to seek out the best writers, materials and resources to secure development.

INTRODUCTION

This unit is part of a series designed to provide you with practical experience of conducting and reporting experimental research. The unit will make use of and build on the knowledge and understanding of the experimental method that you have gained from Unit One. You will be guided through the process of designing and planning two small-scale experiments which should help to extend and consolidate your appreciation of the details of experimental design. You will be asked to test two people for the first experiment and approximately 18 for the second. These exercises have been included to give you some practical experience and the opportunity to observe and talk to the people taking part in an experiment.

A report of the first experiment will be provided to show the material that should go into each section and how the various sections are integrated. You will, with support, be asked to write a full report for the second experiment. This will give you useful practice in preparing reports of experimental research; it will also increase your understanding of how to interpret experimental results. You will need to ask your tutor for feedback on the report that you produce.

Towards the end of the unit you will be given the opportunity to evaluate a published report of a piece of experimental research. Your own first-hand experience of carrying out experimental research should help you to appreciate the issues facing researchers when using the experimental method. Overall, the unit aims to help you both to develop the skills of conducting your own experimental research and the ability and confidence to evaluate the experimental research of others.

As part of the small-scale experiments, you will be asked to summarise and analyse the data that is obtained. This will include carrying out statistical tests. Although some statistical concepts are discussed in the unit, the teaching of statistics is outside the scope of this module. Three strategies have therefore been adopted to help you with the statistical element of the unit.

First, the tests that you do have to carry out have been presented as a series of steps which you can follow by doing a little, very basic arithmetic. Second, a list of three particularly clear and accessible statistics books have been included under Further Reading at the end of the unit. Try to find one that suits you, and use it as a first step in learning about statistics. Third, at various points in the unit, page references have been given to those three books. Although you do not have to refer to any of them in order to complete the exercises, making use of one will help you to consolidate and extend your knowledge and understanding of basic statistical concepts and techniques. You should also note that you will need a calculator for Session Nine.

As in Unit One, all the terms and concepts that are introduced during this unit are highlighted when they first appear in the main body of the text and defined in the margin. The definitions are repeated in the Glossary at the end of the unit. If you are still in doubt about any of the ideas which are discussed, you should consult one of the books that are listed under Further Reading at the end of the unit.

Also as in Unit One, the text contains a number of activities for you to carry out. Although a time allowance has been included for each activity, you should only regard it as a very rough estimate and not be concerned if the activity takes you less or more time than shown.

When you have completed this unit, you will have made considerable progress towards being able to carry out small-scale experimental research. Before you reach that point you will, however, need more research experience with full support and supervision from an experienced tutor. A Masters course or a Diploma in Research Methods, in which you carry out a supervised research project, could be your next step.

Session One discusses research hypotheses and experimental hypotheses. It clarifies the function of the null hypothesis in experimental research and introduces the role of statistical tests. Finally, the term 'theory' is defined and the role of theories explored.

Session Two takes you through the planning of the design of an experiment and the writing of the introduction to an experimental report.

Session Three discusses the detailed preparation for the carrying out of the experiment itself and the collecting of the results. It then describes the method section of an experimental report and gives an example of how it can be written.

Session Four looks at the process of describing and analysing the results of an experiment using descriptive and inferential statistics. It guides you through the process of establishing the level of significance of your results using a sign test and it outlines the requirements of the results section of an experimental report.

Session Five explores the elements required in interpreting the results of an experiment for the discussion section of a report and takes you through a process of interpretation that you may find useful as a model. An example discussion section of a report is also given.

Session Six completes the process of taking you through the writing of an experimental report and gives you a checklist to follow when you are writing your own reports.

Session Seven guides you through a second small-scale experiment so that you can consolidate your learning and practise identifying research questions and planning an experiment.

Session Eight continues to guide you through the second small-scale experiment allowing you the opportunity to practise preparing and conducting an experiment as well as writing the method section of a report.

Session Nine reaches the results section of the experiment and guides you through the organisation and analysis of the data including a different statistical test from the one used earlier. There is also the opportunity to write the results section of the report.

Session Ten uses the plan for the process of interpreting an experiment that was introduced in Session Five and guides you through the writing of the discussion section of the report.

Session Eleven gives you the opportunity to write the final draft of the report which you should give to your tutor for feedback.

Session Twelve asks you to evaluate a published research article and explores some of the issues involved.

Session Thirteen examines the background to the two research styles: qualitative and quantitative; it invites the possibility that both approaches can be used, sometimes side by side.

LEARNING PROFILE

Given below is a list of learning outcomes for each session in this unit. You can use it to identify your current learning, and so to consider how the Unit can help you to develop your knowledge and understanding. The list is not intended to cover all of the details discussed in every session, and so the learning profile should only be used for general guidance.

For each of the learning outcomes listed below, tick the box that corresponds most closely to the point you feel you are at now. This will provide you with an assessment of your current understanding and confidence in the areas that you will study in this unit.

	Not at all	Partly	Quite well	Very well

Session One

I can:
- state when a research hypothesis is necessary ☐ ☐ ☐ ☐
- formulate an experimental hypothesis ☐ ☐ ☐ ☐
- outline the logic of hypothesis testing. ☐ ☐ ☐ ☐

Session Two

I can:
- identify sources of potential research questions ☐ ☐ ☐ ☐
- discuss how to approach the professional literature in a research context ☐ ☐ ☐ ☐
- outline the functions of the sections of a research report ☐ ☐ ☐ ☐
- describe the content and structure of the introduction section of a report. ☐ ☐ ☐ ☐

Session Three

I can:
- make decisions about the procedural details of an experiment ☐ ☐ ☐ ☐
- conduct an experimental procedure with precision ☐ ☐ ☐ ☐
- describe the content and structure of the method section of a report. ☐ ☐ ☐ ☐

Session Four

I can:
- explain the use of descriptive statistics to summarise the findings of an experiment ☐ ☐ ☐ ☐
- interpret the outcome of simple statistical tests ☐ ☐ ☐ ☐
- describe the content and structure of the results section of a report. ☐ ☐ ☐ ☐

	Not at all	Partly	Quite well	Very well

Session Five

I can:

- explain what the interpretation of an experiment involves ☐ ☐ ☐ ☐
- outline how to approach the process of interpretation ☐ ☐ ☐ ☐
- describe the content and structure of the discussion section of a report. ☐ ☐ ☐ ☐

Session Six

I can:

- write a title for a research report ☐ ☐ ☐ ☐
- write an abstract for a research report ☐ ☐ ☐ ☐
- describe the style in which a research report should be written ☐ ☐ ☐ ☐
- prepare a reference list for a research report. ☐ ☐ ☐ ☐

Session Seven

I can:

- describe how past research may generate new research questions ☐ ☐ ☐ ☐
- work out the procedural details for a small-scale experiment ☐ ☐ ☐ ☐
- write the introduction section of an experimental report. ☐ ☐ ☐ ☐

Session Eight

I can:

- conduct a small-scale experimental study ☐ ☐ ☐ ☐
- write the method section of an experimental report. ☐ ☐ ☐ ☐

Session Nine

I can:

- organise and summarise raw data from a small-scale experiment ☐ ☐ ☐ ☐
- select an appropriate statistical test for three or more treatment conditions and carry out the test using data collected ☐ ☐ ☐ ☐
- write the results section of an experimental report. ☐ ☐ ☐ ☐

Session Ten

I can:

- interpret the results of a small-scale experiment ☐ ☐ ☐ ☐
- write the discussion section of an experimental report. ☐ ☐ ☐ ☐

	Not at all	Partly	Quite well	Very well

Session Eleven

I can:
- prepare a complete report of a small-scale experiment ☐ ☐ ☐ ☐
- outline the main reasons for replication of previous experimental research. ☐ ☐ ☐ ☐

Session Twelve

I can:
- read and evaluate published reports of experimental research ☐ ☐ ☐ ☐
- evaluate experimental research to inform professional practice ☐ ☐ ☐ ☐
- synthesise findings from different experiments. ☐ ☐ ☐ ☐

Session Thirteen

I can:
- distinguish between different research paradigms ☐ ☐ ☐ ☐
- discuss how the paradigms might be reconciled ☐ ☐ ☐ ☐
- outline the most appropriate use of the experimental method. ☐ ☐ ☐ ☐

Theories and hypotheses

Introduction

In Unit One: *An Introduction to Experimental Design,* we examined closely many of the decisions that need to be made when designing an experiment and we tried to relate those decisions to the research question originally posed. Although 'specific ideas' and 'predictions' were mentioned, you may have noticed that we did not discuss the issue of the 'research hypothesis'. Since many texts on research methods emphasise the importance of the research hypothesis, you may be wondering how we have managed to get so far without it. In this session we will try to clarify the precise function of the research hypothesis; this should help you to understand how and at what point in the process to formulate a hypothesis. Since there is a close relationship between theories and research hypotheses, we will also examine briefly the nature and uses of theories in this session.

Session objectives

When you have completed this session, you should be able to:

- define and formulate an experimental hypothesis

- identify when in the research process to formulate an experimental hypothesis

- define the null hypothesis

- describe the possible outcomes when a statistical test is applied to numerical data

- discuss the role of theories in experimental research.

1: The research hypothesis and the research process

What is a research hypothesis?

Research hypothesis: *a prediction of the relationship between two or more variables which is stated in a testable form*

Although the whole of this section is aimed at clarifying the idea of a **research hypothesis,** it will be helpful to start with some definitions.

'A hypothesis is a proposition that is stated in testable form and predicts a particular relationship between two (or more) variables.'

(Bailey, 1987)

'A well-constructed hypothesis will meet two criteria.
(1) It will clearly state the relationship between two or more variables.
(2) It will use variables that can potentially be measured.'

(Berger and Patchner, 1988)

'An hypothesis . . . is essentially an intelligent guess about what is happening, but in a form that can be tested.'

(McNeill, 1990)

There is, as you can see, considerable agreement about the definition of a research hypothesis. Essentially, a research hypothesis is the specific prediction that a research study is designed to test. When the study is experimental, the research hypothesis is usually referred to as an **experimental hypothesis.**

Experimental hypothesis: *a prediction of a causal relationship between two or more variables which is stated in a testable form and which will be tested by carrying out an experiment*

Even so, research hypotheses seem to constitute a source of confusion for people studying health care research methods. I have often been asked by students, 'Do I have to have a hypothesis?' or, 'What should my hypothesis be?'. So it seems that hypothesis formation can be perceived as a ritual procedure, entirely separate from the process of identifying research questions and designing studies to answer them.

Research questions and research hypotheses

Research process: *the logical sequence of steps that a researcher must take when carrying out research of any kind*

I suspect that much of the confusion arises from some of the descriptions of the **research process** that are provided in most texts on health care research methods. The term 'research process' is used to describe a list of steps that researchers go through when planning, carrying out and reporting a piece of research. Some authors offer long and very detailed lists, while others summarise the process relatively briefly. For example, Nieswiadomy (1987) identifies 17 steps, whereas Couchman and Dawson (1990) outline seven.

Since the aim of describing the research process is simply to provide a basic checklist for researchers, the actual length of the list should matter little. As the lists become longer and more detailed, however, there is also a tendency for them to become more prescriptive about what constitutes research and precisely how research should be carried out. It is these lengthy lists that seem to cause confusion. One such example is given below.

' 1 Formulating and delimiting the problem.
  2 Reviewing the related literature.
  3 Developing a theoretical framework.
  4 Formulating a research hypothesis.
  5 Selecting a research design.
  6 Specifying the population.
  7 Selecting methods to measure the research variable.

8   Conducting a pilot study.

9   Selecting the sample.

10   Collecting the data.

11   Preparing the data for analysis.

12   Analysing the data.

13   Interpreting the results.

14   Communicating the findings.'

(Polit and Hungler, 1989)

ACTIVITY I   ALLOW 15 MINUTES

For this activity you can either use the research questions that we identified in Session One of Unit One, or you can think up some new examples.

1   Identify a *predictive* research question and then read carefully through steps 1 to 9 of Polit and Hungler's description of the research process given above. Imagine that you are going to use the steps to guide your actions in planning the research. Note down any items in the list which might cause problems for you.

2   Identify a *descriptive* research question and repeat the process, again noting down any items in the list which might cause you problems.

Commentary

I encountered a number of problems when I tried to imagine putting this description of the research process into action. Specifically, they were as follows:

1   The predictive research question I came up with was, 'Is the mouth care of patients improved by using a toothbrush instead of gauze or cotton wool?'. In this example I felt that I had formulated the problem clearly and that it did not need delimiting. The idea of reviewing the literature did not pose any real difficulty either.

The next two steps, however, presented some major problems. First, I could not envisage any possible relevant theoretical framework. Second, I felt in no position to state a research hypothesis until I had decided what sort of study I would carry out and the precise details of that study. Although I would probably choose to do an experiment comparing the effects of toothbrushes and gauze, I would still need to decide how to measure improvements in mouth care. Without this decision I could not formulate an experimental hypothesis since it must be stated in testable terms. Further, I might have to revise the research question during the design process and so there seems little reason to formulate the hypothesis at this early stage. I felt that, in principle, I could use the remaining steps to guide the planning of the research.

2   The descriptive research question I arrived at was, 'How do health care practitioners cope with their own grief and loss experienced in the course of professional practice?'. Although I felt clear about the nature of the problem and was prepared to consult the existing literature, I wanted to approach the issue with as few preconceptions as possible. In other words, it was neither possible nor desirable to develop a theoretical framework or to formulate a research hypothesis. Two other steps which gave me problems were 6 and 9. I was more interested in developing my understanding of the issue than in generalising my findings from a sample to a population. I was also unsure about step 7 since I did not really have a research or dependent variable in the strict sense of the term.

You may have noticed that for both of the questions in the activity, the idea of developing a theoretical framework seemed rather unclear; we will be discussing this issue in more detail in the final section of this session. Two important questions concerning research hypotheses have, however, emerged from the activity. These are:

- the kind of research question for which a hypothesis is needed

- the point during the research process at which a research hypothesis can be formulated.

These two issues will be dealt with in turn. First, it is important to note that research hypotheses are not obligatory for all research. Because descriptive research questions essentially ask 'What is the case?', no predictions can or should be made in advance of the research. Accounts of the research process which include formulating a research hypothesis as an essential step are, therefore, rather misleading.

Research hypotheses are associated with *predictive* rather than *descriptive* research questions. In order to clarify this point, the nature of that association needs to be made more explicit. Can you remember the definition that was given of predictive research questions in Unit One? They were characterised as a broad category of research questions which contain specific ideas or predictions that can be tested through research. The examples that were given were:

'Does routine weighing alleviate any anxiety?'
'Does routine weighing make any anxiety worse?'
'Are there any benefits to infants of restricting women's weight
gain in pregnancy?'

The predictions that these questions contain can be thought of as embryonic research hypotheses. In other words, research hypotheses are not tacked on to predictive research questions as an afterthought or optional extra, they are already implicit in the way in which the research questions are phrased. All experimental research, therefore, tests a hypothesis.

Formulating an experimental hypothesis

Although research hypotheses are associated with predictive research questions, the two are clearly not identical. This being the case, it is necessary, as was noted above, to identify the point at which a research hypothesis should be formulated. Although Polit and Hungler (1989) suggest that this should be a relatively early step in the research process, you may have noted some problems in Activity 1 in trying to follow that advice. The issues should become clearer if we compare predictive research questions with research hypotheses. Look back to the definitions of research hypotheses given at the beginning of this session and try to identify the differences between the prediction implied in a research question and a research hypothesis.

Research hypotheses differ from the predictions made in research questions in two important ways. Research hypotheses state:

- the precise predicted relationship between two (or more) variables

- in measurable terms.

Thus, the predictive research question, 'Does routine weighing make any anxiety worse?' might become an experimental hypothesis such as:

'Women who are weighed at every antenatal visit will express more worry or anxiety to health care practitioners during their antenatal care than women who are not weighed at all.'

Both 'routine weighing' and 'anxiety' have been expressed in measurable terms; in other words, the actual concrete procedures or operations that would have to be carried out have been specified. As you may recall from Unit One, this is known as providing an operational definition. Thus, stating a predicted relationship between two (or more) variables in measurable terms necessarily involves operationally defining those variables.

In experimental research, the 'predicted cause' in a research question is operationally defined when you construct the independent variable; the 'supposed effect' is operationally defined in order to specify the dependent variable or variables. Thus, an experimental hypothesis states the predicted relationship between the independent and dependent variables.

You may wonder why the comparison 'than women who are not weighed at all' was included in the hypothesis. If it had not been, then only one variable (anxiety) would have been identified and no relationship could have been predicted. 'Women who are weighed at every antenatal visit' is not a variable until it is contrasted with another condition involving less frequent weighing or no weighing at all. An experimental hypothesis must, therefore, include the different treatment conditions or levels of the independent variable.

Use the activity below to gain some practice in writing experimental hypotheses.

ACTIVITY 2 — ALLOW 10 MINUTES

Given below is a list of predictive research questions. Formulate an experimental hypothesis which might be derived from each of them. You will have to make up some details of the study in order to write the hypotheses.

1 Does individualised patient care in hospitals affect rate of recovery?

2 Do health care students who take research methods courses make use of research findings to guide professional practice?

3 Do women who attend antenatal classes experience less pain in labour?

4 Does giving a young baby extra milk at the last feed of the day help to ensure a peaceful night for the parents?

Which, if any, of your hypotheses do you think should be tested by partial rather than true experiments?

Commentary

A number of different hypotheses could be derived from each of these questions. Some possibilities are given below.

1 Patients who receive individualised care while in hospital will differ in length of stay in hospital from patients who receive more task-orientated care.

2 Health care students who have taken a research methods course will be able to cite more instances of the use of research findings to guide practice than health care students who have not.

3 Women who attend antenatal classes throughout pregnancy will request less analgesia during labour than women who do not attend at all.

4 Breast-fed three-month-old babies who are given two extra ounces of milk at the last feed will have longer periods of uninterrupted sleep than infants who do not receive the supplement.

Although all of these hypotheses are experimental, partial experiments would probably be needed for (2) and (3) since ethical and practical considerations would prohibit the random allocation of women to antenatal class attendance or students to courses.

You may have been surprised by the suggested hypothesis for (1). It is important to note that experimental hypotheses do not always predict the direction of an effect. The independent variable may be expected simply to give rise to a difference between the treatment conditions, and this expectation is reflected in the hypothesis. When this is the case the hypothesis is labelled **two-tailed**. If a hypothesis predicts the direction of an effect it is known as a **one-tailed hypothesis**.

Two-tailed hypothesis: *this predicts a relationship between two (or more) variables*

One-tailed hypothesis: *this predicts a relationship between two (or more) variables in a particular direction*

We have seen that research hypotheses are implied by, and can be derived from, predictive research questions. Even so, no research question can dictate the design to be adopted and so hypotheses cannot be formulated before design decisions have been made. In an experimental study you cannot state your prediction in measurable terms until you have specified the independent variable and how it will be varied, and identified the dependent variable or variables to be used. Polit and Hungler's (1989) description of the research process seems to suggest that you proceed from the research question to the hypothesis and only then to the research design. You will, I believe, find it easier when planning an experiment to concentrate on the research question and the experimental design. The decisions you make will determine the experimental hypothesis – stating it precisely should be thought of as one of the last steps before actually carrying out the experiment.

We have now considered how to arrive at a hypothesis; the question we have not examined is why you need one. Why not just forget about the hypothesis and proceed to try to answer the research question? In an experiment, the hypothesis gives a precise prediction which can be tested against what actually happens. These points will be considered in more detail below.

2: Hypothesis testing

The uses of experimental hypotheses

Can you see any advantages in formulating a clear and unambiguous experimental hypothesis? Given that we have placed the formulation of a hypothesis at a relatively late stage in the design process, it can serve to summarise and highlight some of the important design decisions you have made. Sometimes when you have to write a precise prediction of what you expect to find, you realise that you have strayed further than you intended from your original question. Certainly, if you discover that you cannot state a clear hypothesis before you start your actual experiment, then you should check your experimental design very carefully.

Even more important, however, is that a clear experimental hypothesis helps a clear conclusion to be drawn from the findings of a study. You may recall that both Bailey (1987) and McNeill (1990) stressed that a hypothesis should be *testable*.

By testable, they mean not only that the variables can be measured in some way, but also that the findings should clearly either support or refute the hypothesis. If there is no experimental hypothesis, or if the hypothesis is stated in very vague terms, then unproductive arguments can arise between researchers who claim that the findings support their prediction and critics who claim that they do not. Take, for example, the research hypothesis that, 'Premature infants who receive breast milk will do better than premature infants who receive a milk formula'. What results would support this hypothesis? What results would refute it? What does 'do better' mean anyway? You might have to wait until the participants are middle-aged before you could reach a decision.

In experimental research it is the hypothesis and not the research question that is tested against reality; that is to say, against what is actually happening. If no clear prediction is made, then no clear test of that prediction can be achieved. The clarity of the prediction is, therefore, more essential than the objectivity of the findings: although numerical data are more usually collected, comments, views, opinions and feelings can also be used to support or refute an experimental hypothesis.

The null hypothesis

Thus, the formulation of a precise hypothesis allows for a clear conclusion to be drawn from a study; it does not, however, guarantee it. In Unit One, Session Five it was noted that, because of extraneous variables, numerical findings are rarely clear cut. Do you remember the example of the pea seeds when a single extraneous variable was introduced – the germination potential of the seeds? The results looked like this:

	Condition 5 degrees	Condition 15 degrees	Condition 30 degrees
	2	4	2
	5	7	5
	5	4	5
	5	7	2
	5	7	2
Mean =	4.4	5.8	3.2

However clear the prediction, these findings might have occurred by chance alone; we cannot be sure if the observed difference is due to the temperature or to random error. In order to estimate the likelihood or probability that the observed differences are due to chance factors, we would have to carry out a statistical test. When an experimental research study produces numerical findings, then the hypothesis can only be supported or refuted statistically.

There is, though, one further complication. A statistical test does not test the experimental hypothesis directly, it tests instead a statistical device called the **null hypothesis** (see Clegg, 1982, pp. 59–61; Greene, 1990, p. 3 and p. 27; Caulcott, 1992, pp. 129–136). In experimental research the null hypothesis states that the independent variable exerts no effect on the treatment conditions. This does not imply that the conditions will be identical in any particular study, but that whatever effect is observed is due entirely to random error.

When a statistical test is applied to numerical data, one of two broad outcomes can be obtained:

1   There is a very small likelihood or probability that the findings were due to random error alone. The effects are then referred to as 'significant'. In this

Null hypothesis: *a statistical hypothesis which is evaluated and assessed in statistical analyses. The null hypothesis states that the independent variable exerts no effect and therefore that any difference between conditions in a given study has arisen by chance alone*

case, we *can reject* the null hypothesis although we have not totally disproved it; there is still some possibility that random error was responsible.

2   There is a considerable likelihood or probability that the findings were due entirely to random error. The effects are then referred to as 'nonsignificant'. In this case we *cannot reject* the null hypothesis; however, we cannot fully accept it either. The independent variable may have an effect which our experimental procedure was too insensitive to detect. If the experiment were to be repeated with more accurate measurement, for example, then the effects of the independent variable might be more clearly shown.

The fate of the null hypothesis directly determines the fate of the experimental hypothesis. Let's consider, then, what conclusions can be drawn about the experimental hypothesis from the two possible outcomes outlined above. Read carefully through the following scenario and then try the two activities which follow it.

> An experiment is set up to evaluate the effectiveness of a set of dietary instructions on the weight control of men and women aged between 40 and 60 years. The experimental hypothesis is that people who are given the dietary instructions will gain less weight than people to whom the instructions are not made available.
>
> At the end of the study the two sets of weight gains are collected. The people who received the dietary instructions seem, on average, to have gained less weight than those who did not. The weight gains in the two conditions are compared using an appropriate statistical test.

ACTIVITY 3   ALLOW 5 MINUTES

As a result of carrying out the statistical test, the researchers discover that there is a very small likelihood that the difference is due to random error alone. They can, therefore, reject the null hypothesis. What do you think they can say about the experimental hypothesis?

Commentary

Although the null hypothesis can be rejected, this does not exclude the possibility (however small) that the difference is due entirely to random error. The best that the researchers can say, therefore, is that the results of the statistical test support the experimental hypothesis. They cannot regard it as proved or established beyond any shadow of doubt.

Further, and perhaps even more importantly, although the researchers can now accept that the observed difference is unlikely to be due to chance, they still have not isolated the actual cause of the difference. They may, for example, have given more attention to the weight of people receiving the dietary instructions and so confounded the experiment. The fact that the experimental hypothesis is supported does not mean that the independent variable is necessarily responsible. Now consider the second possible outcome.

ACTIVITY 4   ALLOW 5 MINUTES

As a result of carrying out the statistical test, the researchers discover that there is a considerable likelihood that the difference was due to chance factors alone. They cannot, therefore, reject the null hypothesis. What do you think they can say about the experimental hypothesis?

Commentary

Because there is still a possibility (however small) that the difference between the conditions is 'genuine', the experimental hypothesis cannot be said to have been disproved. The result of the statistical test may not provide support for the experimental hypothesis, but it cannot conclusively demonstrate that it is false.

Furthermore, although the researchers must accept in this case that any differences may be due to chance alone, they still cannot be sure why that result was obtained. Perhaps, for example, the weighing device that was used was rather unreliable. An experiment may not be sensitive enough to detect any differences, although the independent variable may nonetheless have had an effect.

So you need to remember that when numerical data are gathered, the experimental hypothesis is evaluated statistically. Statistical procedures do not directly examine the truth or falsity of the experimental hypothesis; they estimate instead the likelihood or probability that the results have been obtained by chance alone. Furthermore, even if there is a very small likelihood that the results have been obtained by chance, the role of the independent variable as a causal factor is not fully established.

Self-assessment questions

1   Do you have to have a hypothesis in order to carry out research?

2   Is the following statement a research hypothesis? If not, why not?

    'I think that sodium intake affects blood pressure.'

3   Why do researchers never 'accept' the null hypothesis?

4   If the null hypothesis is rejected, does this mean that changes in the independent variable must be responsible for any effects observed?

3: The role of theory

What is a theory?

In Activity 1 we noted that the idea of 'developing a theoretical framework' as part of the research process seemed rather unclear. Were you sure precisely what was meant by this phrase? It is of course somewhat unfair to examine the proposed steps in the research process independently of the supporting text. Polit and Hungler (1989) do, in fact, provide a detailed discussion in a later chapter of what they mean by a **theoretical framework** which you might like to have a look at (see Further Reading). In many cases in health care research literature, however, the terms 'theoretical framework' or '**theory**' are used without any definition being

Theoretical framework: *a view of events provided by a theory*

Theory: *a theory summarises and integrates existing knowledge, and, in doing so, suggests new predictions that can be made*

offered. Draper (1990), for example, explores four different roles for theory in nursing, but does not define 'theory' at any point. Do you feel clear about the terms 'theory' and 'theoretical framework'?

Bailey (1987) points out that there are a number of different conceptions of theory. Two can readily be seen in everyday usage. First, we may talk about a very impractical idea as 'theoretically possible' but 'practically impossible'. In this sense 'theoretically' means 'in principle' and this is very different from its usage in research. Second, we may say 'I'm not sure what happened, but I do have a theory'. In this case, theory is being used to describe a possible but untested explanation. This second instance is much closer to the way in which researchers use the term 'theory', but in a research context there is an additional requirement that the explanation should be *testable*.

Explanations and predictions

We can clarify the term 'theory' further by looking at the way in which researchers make use of theories. Theories have two interrelated roles: they provide possible explanations and they provide predictions. Let's have a look at each of these in turn.

1 Theories as explanations

Research studies that are carried out produce findings of various kinds, but the findings often need to be explained. So, for example, it has been suggested that:

- the risk of cot death is associated with ethnicity (Gantley, Davies and Murcott, 1993)

- coping devices taught to patients can reduce reported pain (Boore, 1978)

- some patients are not popular with nursing staff (Stockwell, 1972).

Although such findings may be very valuable in their own right, it is also possible to offer explanations or theories for them. For the examples above the kind of theories that might be offered are:

- the risk of cot death is associated with ethnicity because young babies in some ethnic groups are left to sleep on their own in a quiet environment

- coping devices taught to patients can reduce reported pain because they give the patient a feeling of control over events

- some patients are not popular with nursing staff because they do not confirm the role of the nurse.

Theories are not discovered by researchers; rather they are created by researchers or by anybody else who has access to the findings. Theories rest on research observations and findings, but they go beyond them in order to offer possible explanations of events and relationships that have been observed.

2 Theories and predictions

You may have realised that all the explanations or theories offered above could be tested; that is, although they cannot be tested directly, they give rise to testable predictions. The theory about cot death, for example, leads to the prediction that a noisier environment would reduce the risk. In principle, this could be examined by, for instance, leaving a radio on in the room.

ACTIVITY 5

ALLOW 5 MINUTES

Re-read the other two theories offered above and note down at least one testable prediction that can be derived from each of them. Remember that you are aiming to test the theory, not just to collect more findings.

Commentary

I came up with the following:

Coping devices
The theory suggests that it is perceived control which is important. Other methods of helping patients to feel in control could be examined.

Popularity of patients with nurses
The theory suggests that any event which fails to confirm the role of the nurse would be disliked. Changes in hospital procedures could be examined from this perspective.

Because theories give rise to testable predictions, they can provide a valuable spur for new research. They can also help you to look at events in a different way and from a different perspective. It is worth noting, however, that no matter how much positive support is obtained for a particular theory, it cannot be said to be *proved*. New evidence can always appear and demonstrate that the theory is false or inadequate in some way.

You may be feeling slightly confused at this point since the term 'theory' is not only often used without being defined, but is also used rather broadly. Orem's (1985) ideas about self-care and different types of nursing systems are, for example, often referred to as a theory. Yet Orem offers a classification of nursing activities rather than an explanation of an observed relationship between variables as we saw in the theories given above. So Orem's theory is perhaps better characterised as a **model** or a **conceptual framework** in that it provides a way of viewing professional practice.

You should also recognise that theories are not the only source of testable predictions: ideas, predictions and hypotheses can be drawn from a number of sources. For instance, questioning the effectiveness of specific procedures or therapies in your own area of work is one useful source of ideas.

So, although Polit and Hungler's (1989) description of the research process implies that 'developing a theoretical framework' is a necessary step, this is clearly not strictly true. Further, as was pointed out above, research findings may be useful and important in their own right without the need for theoretical explanations.

If you have carried out a piece of research, experimental or not, it is worth thinking carefully about possible explanations for the findings. If you can use your knowledge and understanding to propose a theoretical explanation, then you may broaden the potential application of your research. The explanation that was proposed for Stockwell's (1972) findings, for example, could lead to an understanding of nurses' feelings about their role which would have implications beyond the issue of the 'unpopular' patient.

Model: *a representation, often in the form of a diagram, of some aspect of behaviour or the environment*

Conceptual framework: *a way of viewing or classifying events or behaviour*

Summary

1   It is not obligatory to have a hypothesis in order to carry out research. Research hypotheses are implicit in the way in which predictive research questions are phrased.

2   Because experimental hypotheses involve specifying the independent and dependent variables precisely, they are most readily formulated once the experiment has been designed.

3   Experimental hypotheses must be testable in the sense that they will be either supported or refuted by the results obtained.

4   Statistical testing of the null hypothesis provides an estimate of the likelihood that any effects have been caused entirely by random error. This does not reveal why significant effects have or have not been obtained; confounding or lack of sensitivity may be responsible.

5   Theories provide explanations and predictions by building on observations and findings.

Before you move on to Session Two, check that you have achieved the objectives given at the beginning of this session, and, if not, review the appropriate sections.

SESSION TWO

Planning a small-scale experiment

Introduction

We have so far discussed and summarised the steps that need to be taken when designing a piece of experimental research, and you made use of that knowledge and understanding to read and evaluate two reports of experimental research at the end of Unit One. You have not yet, however, had the opportunity to put your knowledge into practice and to design and conduct an experimental study yourself. In this session we will begin the process of planning and carrying out a small experiment to help you to consolidate and extend the skills that you have acquired.

Session objectives

When you have completed this session, you should be able to:

- describe various ways to identify a potential research question

- outline the steps required to decide on an experimental design

- draft the introduction to an experimental report.

1: Finding a research question

The research process

As we have seen, the starting point for any piece of research is a question of some kind. Although different accounts of the research process may vary quite considerably, there seems to be little dispute over the notion that research must begin from a specific question. Furthermore, most authors on research methods agree that the next step in the research process is to consult the research literature. Given below are some examples of the first two steps in the research process as identified by a number of different authors.

'1 Deciding on the research question
 2 Locating and searching relevant literature'

(Burnard and Morrison, 1990)

'1 Formulating and delimiting the problem
 2 Reviewing the related literature'

(Polit and Hungler, 1989)

'1 Defining the problem
 2 Searching the literature'

(Clifford and Gough, 1990)

'1 Asking the research question
 2 Searching the literature'

(Cormack, 1991)

'1 Stating research problem or question
 2 Reviewing relevant literature'

(Couchman and Dawson, 1990)

It may seem rather self-evident that you cannot embark on the process of research unless you have some idea about what you want to know, and that you then have to check out the relevant literature in order to discover what work has been done so far. Nonetheless, these initial steps are not quite as mechanical or automatic as they may sound.

Sources of research questions

First, you need to think about *how* interesting and worthwhile research questions can be generated. The following activity asks you to think about the possible sources of research questions that we have identified so far.

ACTIVITY 6   ALLOW 15 MINUTES

Look back over the sessions you have studied so far in both units and note down any sources of research questions that have been identified. Add as many other possibilities to your list as you can think of.

Commentary

In Unit One, Session One, we generated research questions simply by taking an aspect of professional practice and listing any doubts or queries to which it gave rise. Your own professional experience can be a highly productive source of research questions, not least because you are very familiar with the ideas, concepts and procedures involved.

When we discussed theories and hypotheses in Session One of this unit, an alternative source of research questions was implicitly identified. As we noted, theoretical explanations provide predictions that can be tested through research. For example, one theory we identified was that, 'coping devices taught to patients can reduce reported pain because they give the patients a feeling of control over events'. It was suggested that other ways of helping patients to feel in control should, according to this theory, also be effective. Can you think of any possibilities? If you can, then you have the basis for a research question which is derived directly from a theoretical explanation and provides a test of that explanation.

Theories not only give rise to testable predictions, but can also provide ideas for further studies. You might, for instance, have wondered if helping the patients or clients that you work with to feel more in control of their treatment and care could have beneficial effects. You might also be able to think of ways in which you could research this idea.

In a similar way, models and conceptual frameworks can suggest ideas for research into aspects of professional practice. Draper (1990) suggests that models of nursing can fulfil four distinct roles. They are to:

- define nursing by describing nursing phenomena
- form a realistic basis for curriculum design
- provide tools for the professional practice of nursing
- provide a language with which nurses can discuss nursing.

Thus, models of practice can help you to think closely about the nature of your professional activities and so give rise to useful and relevant research. As Butterworth (1991) points out, research of this kind is of crucial importance in areas such as mental health nursing in which massive policy changes have recently taken place.

You may well have some other ideas on your list of sources of research questions, and might like to compare it with suggestions made by other authors. Cormack (1991), for example, identifies five possible sources. They are as follows:

- your own experience
- professional literature
- theoretical frameworks
- conferences and study days
- national directives and Delphi studies.

Delphi studies involve collecting and analysing the judgements of a group of experts, such as health care practitioners, on a specific question or issue. Reid (1989) provides a useful description and evaluation of this approach.

The professional literature

How did your list compare to Cormack's? The major item that we have neglected so far is the professional literature. Cormack also suggests, as do many other authors, that previously published research can provide a useful source of research questions. You might, for example, try to **replicate** an interesting finding in a slightly different setting and with another group of participants. Such research can be extremely useful and results which have not been replicated should not be used as a basis for professional practice.

This suggestion brings us, however, to a problem that may be encountered in starting a piece of research; namely, that becoming involved with the professional literature can seem like quite a formidable task. The difficulty is particularly

To replicate: *to repeat a study precisely as it is reported in a similar situation with similar participants. Replications act as a check on the reliability of the original findings*

relevant to experimental research. In order to design an experimental study, you must be able to put forward a plausible and worthwhile prediction. To formulate such a prediction, you must have a detailed knowledge of the subject area. Although that knowledge can in part be derived from professional practice (for instance, you have observed that two events seem to be related and want to test the idea systematically), you should also have a clear understanding of previous research in the area.

We have identified two points at which the relevant literature may be consulted. It may, as Cormack and others suggest, serve as a source of research questions, or it may constitute the second step in the research process. In either case, you should approach the literature in a systematic and organised way. If you feel daunted by this prospect or you are unsure about how to make use of the literature, then you might like to have a look at *Research Awareness, Module 4: Searching the Literature* (Roddham, 1989). You might also find it useful to consider the following suggestions:

1   Individual research articles can be used as a basis for further research, but try to avoid diving cold into the literature in the search for a research question. If you already have some ideas about your possible research question when you consult the literature, it will give structure and purpose to your reading. You should, though, be prepared to revise your question in the light of what you find.

2   Do not despair if you encounter conflicting findings. Reviewing and comparing various studies can be an interesting and important project in its own right. Brown, Meikle and Webb (1991), for example, report a detailed and systematic analysis of research articles published between 1956 and 1989 on the collection of mid-stream specimens of urine. Because no clear guidelines for practice emerged, the project underlined the need for further careful research in the area.

3   Many discussions of the research process seem to suggest that you can follow the steps entirely on your own. I believe that this gives a false impression. When you are just starting out on research, you need someone to help you to evaluate your research question and to guide you through previous research. A research supervisor will not only enable you to acquire the skills of research, but should also be very familiar with the research topic in which you are interested and so help you to make sense of the relevant literature.

In this unit, rather than suggesting that you undertake a piece of original experimental research, you will be asked to carry out two research practicals. The aim is to develop your understanding of the experimental method while bypassing some of the steps in the research process. The research question for the first practical and some of the relevant literature are described in the next section. We will then work from the research question to the design of the experiment.

2: From a research question to an experimental design

Identifying the research question

Most nurses, midwives and health visitors spend a substantial amount of time giving information to patients and clients about aspects of health care. There is, however, a considerable wealth of evidence which suggests that much of this information is forgotten even when it is initially understood. Ley (1988) points out that this problem occurs even with information that patients need in order to give informed consent to medical procedures.

Not all information is, however, equally likely to be forgotten. Items which are presented first tend to be remembered best. This is known as a **primacy effect** and it is a common finding in studies of human memory. Wattley and Müller (1984) describe a practical that they carried out on this topic with a class of 14 nursing students. A list of 15 anatomical items was read out to the students and they were then asked to recall as many items as they could within a 45 second period. The mean recall rate dropped from 100 per cent for the second item to 21 per cent for the seventh.

Primacy effect: *a term used to describe the finding that items which are presented first in a list of items tend to be recalled best*

Can you see any limitations to this study? Although a clear primacy effect was demonstrated, the experiment may have lacked ecological validity. In other words, memory for health care information, which is usually given as a series of related statements, may be rather different from memory for single words. Thus, the question which we will investigate in our practical is 'Does order of presentation affect memory for a series of statements which convey health care information?'.

Which research method?

Is this a descriptive or a predictive research question? Because it contains a specific idea it can be labelled 'predictive'. The prediction is that order of presentation will cause a change in memory for the information. The most direct method of testing the prediction is experimental. Can you think of any other research method that could be used? I cannot. Even if recall of patients or clients in a real-life situation were examined, it would still be a **field experiment**. This point will become clearer once we have considered the design of the study. Because of ethical and practical constraints, we will carry out what Ley (1988) calls an **analogue study**. In other words, our participants will be healthy volunteers rather than patients or clients. Can you think of any limitations which this strategy might impose on the interpretation of our results?

Field experiment: *an experiment which is carried out in a real-life situation*

Analogue study: *a term used by Ley (1988) to describe studies carried out with healthy volunteers which are intended to resemble health care situations in most relevant respects*

The next task is to design the experiment and for this we will follow the decision chart that we drew up in Unit One, Session Nine. The activities below will help you to make use of that chart to decide the features of an actual study. The details of what statements and procedure to use will be covered in the next session.

Specifying and varying the independent variable

ACTIVITY 7   ALLOW 5 MINUTES

The research question is 'Does order of presentation affect memory for a series of statements which convey health care information?'.

Note down the predicted cause in this question. Specify the independent variable and decide how it might be varied in the experiment.

Commentary

The predicted cause in the research question has been underlined.

'Does <u>order of presentation</u> affect memory for a series of statements which convey health care information?'

This predicted cause translates directly into an independent variable which is 'order of presentation of statements in the list'. You may have found it quite difficult to see how to vary this independent variable. In effect, all you need to do is to set up a list of statements as one group of statements or items will necessarily come early in the list and another group later. Thus, different 'types' of position have been arranged. To keep things simple, we can therefore regard the experiment as having two different treatment conditions. These are:

Condition 1 – Early items
Condition 2 – Late items

Because this independent variable is necessarily manipulated any time a list of statements is presented, a real-life situation in which a patient or client is given health care information could, in principle, be used for a field experiment.

Treatment conditions and people

The research question implies that we want to draw general conclusions about memory, so we will need a representative sample. How big do you think that sample needs to be? Many studies have shown that, although memory ability may vary between individuals, most people are susceptible to primacy effects. Quite a small sample might, therefore, be reasonably representative of people in general. In this practical, the sample of participants has been drawn for you. It consists of 18 students on a variety of different courses and these results will be provided. You will be asked, however, to obtain results from a further two participants in order that you can have the experience of going through the procedure for yourself.

The next step is to decide whether the same or different people are to experience the two treatment conditions.

ACTIVITY 8   ALLOW 5 MINUTES

Two treatment conditions have been outlined. They are:

Condition 1 – Early items
Condition 2 – Late items

Are the same or different people going to experience the two conditions? Note down your decision and any implications which you believe it has for sample size.

Commentary

This may have seemed a rather obvious question, but it is always worth thinking your way carefully and systematically through the different design features.

Since items cannot be experienced as 'early' or 'late' unless all items are experienced, it is inevitable that the same subjects will take part in both treatment conditions. In other words, we will use a repeated-measures design. This being the case, we need a smaller sample than would be required for an independent-groups design – we will be able to get two scores from every individual.

When you use a repeated-measures design, as we are in this practical, you have to consider the possibility of order effects. In other words, you have to think whether the treatment conditions might produce different results simply because one is experienced before the other. You may recall from Session Three in Unit One that the solution to this problem is to counterbalance the order of presentation of the conditions so that half of the participants experience condition 1 followed by condition 2 and vice versa for the other half. Do we need to worry about order effects in this study? Fortunately not – in our case it is the order effects which are the subject of the investigation.

Control of extraneous variables

The next step is to consider any extraneous variables that need to be controlled. Use the following activity to see what you can come up with.

ACTIVITY 9 ALLOW 10 MINUTES

Make a list of any extraneous variables that you can think of that need to be controlled. You might find it helpful to divide your list into variables relating to participants and variables relating to the situation. Remember that extraneous variables can:

- confound an experiment by varying systematically with the independent variable

- increase random error and so obscure the effects of the independent variable.

Consider, for example, the characteristics of the participants and any instructions which might be given to them.

Commentary

The ideas that I came up with are given below.

Participants
As was noted above, we are going to use a repeated-measures design. There is, therefore, no possibility that the two conditions will vary systematically in terms of the people experiencing them.

Any decision to restrict the sample in any way (e.g. to a particular age group) would have to be made at the sampling stage. The sample in this study was in fact restricted to people aged between 25 and 42 years old and so it may not be possible to generalise the findings to an older or a younger population.

Situation
Some possibilities are:
- instructions given to the participants
- time of day
- level of noise in the environment
- memorability of statements in the list
- rate of presentation of statements.

Did you think of anything else? Which of these extraneous variables do you think should be held constant? I suggest that the instructions given, the rate of presentation and the level of noise should all be held constant as far as possible. The time of day is unlikely to exert a large effect on the pattern of results and can safely be left to vary.

The statements in the list present slightly more of a problem. Clearly, items in the two different list positions must vary and, this being the case, there is the possibility that some items might be more memorable than others. In this way, the actual statements used might confound the experiment. To deal with this possibility the same statements will be used for all participants, but the first group of items and the last group of items will be swapped for half of the participants.

As you can see, we have made every effort to ensure that the study is internally valid. What effects do you think our precautions might have on the ecological validity? There is the danger that we have created a situation which is very different from the one to which we want to generalise our findings. Perhaps, for example, in a noisier environment with more anxious people very different results would be obtained. For this reason, it is very important to consider the results of analogue studies alongside the findings from field experiments.

Measurement of the effect

The dependent variable we will use is the recall of items from the list. The list of statements will be read to participants, and, after a delay, they will be asked to recall as many as possible in whatever order they choose. In order to compare the early items with the later ones, we will regard the first six items as 'early' and the last six as 'late'.

Self-assessment question

5   What scale of measurement is being used?

Overall, our design is now as follows:

	Stage 1	Stage 2	Stage 3
Condition 1 – Early items	Items read aloud to participants	Delay	Free recall of items
Condition 2 – Late items	Items read aloud to participants	Delay	Free recall of items

Stating the experimental hypothesis

We are now in a position to note down a precise prediction or experimental hypothesis. Have a try.

ACTIVITY 10   ALLOW 5 MINUTES

Write down an experimental hypothesis for the study we have designed. Bear in mind that, although hypotheses do not have to predict the direction of the effect, in this case we already have plenty of evidence to suggest that early items will be remembered better than later ones, and therefore you may wish to predict the direction of the effect.

Commentary

My version of the experimental hypothesis is:

'Participants will be able to recall more initial statements giving health care information than later statements'.

Review of the experimental design

We have now mapped out the essential features of the design of our experiment and made a clear, testable prediction. If we obtain a difference between the two conditions, then we should be able to attribute the cause of the difference to the list position. If we do not obtain a difference, it will cast some doubt on the idea that there are primacy effects in the recall of statements about health care information.

The important item that we have so far neglected is to decide exactly how the data will be analysed – which statistical test or tests will be used to examine any difference that is obtained. The omission is deliberate since we are not ready to consider statistics at this stage, but it is important to recognise that analyses of the results are usually planned as an experiment is designed and not after the data have been collected.

Although some details are yet to be described, we are now in a position where we can begin to write the report of the research. It is tempting to postpone writing a report until after the experiment is complete, but if you do so, there is a real danger that you will lose track of some of the detail and of your line of reasoning. I will therefore adopt the strategy of writing each section as soon as possible. We will begin now with the introduction.

3: Writing an experimental report - the introduction

Components of an experimental report

Even if you have not yet tried your hand at writing a report of an experiment, you have certainly read some and this experience will be of considerable help to you. Let us start by having a brief look at the basic ingredients of an experimental report.

ACTIVITY 11 ALLOW **15** MINUTES

Go back to the two experimental reports which were included as Resources 3 and 4 in Unit One. They are the articles by Holden, Sagovsky and Cox (1989) and Sleep and Grant (1987). Make a list of the different sections that are contained in each report and note briefly what you believe to be the function of each section. Why, for example, do you think an abstract is included?

Commentary

These two experimental reports are typical in terms of the sections they contain. The sections are as follows:

- Title
- Abstract
- Introduction
- Methods/Subjects and Methods
- Findings/Results
- Discussion
- References.

Since we will be discussing the function and presentation of each of these sections in detail in later sessions, I will give only a very brief statement on each at this point.

Title
This should indicate precisely the topic that is being investigated.

Abstract
This is intended to provide a brief summary of what was done, what was found and any conclusions drawn. It allows readers to decide if the paper is of interest to them and whether or not to read further.

Introduction
The aim of this section is to provide the rationale for the study.

Method
This section should provide sufficient detail to allow the study to be replicated.

Results
The analyses of the findings are presented in this section. The analyses should provide a clear test of the hypothesis, but no interpretation of the findings is given here.

Discussion
The aim of this section is to draw conclusions from the analyses of the results. Ideas which were raised in the introduction are reconsidered in the light of the findings.

References
Here there must be a complete list of all sources such as books and articles to which reference has been made.

The functions of each of the sections should provide some clues as to when each section can be written. The abstract, although it comes first in the report, is usually the last item to be written. The introduction can, however, be written before the experiment is actually carried out. It is, in effect, a statement of what you intend to do and why you intend to do it. For this reason, your study is described in the introduction using the future tense.

The introduction

The single most important point to remember about an introduction is that it is not an essay. This may sound rather obvious to you, but many practical reports are written using the 'ham sandwich' model. The introduction and discussion appear to be two rather unrelated essays on the topic with which the experiment is concerned, and the experiment itself is a sort of filler between the two. Do bear in mind that although a report is divided into sections, each of the sections must be firmly linked to form a coherent and integrated whole.

Coolican (1990) provides a very useful way of thinking about the introduction to an experimental report. He suggests that it should be rather like a funnel. Thus:

Start with the general subject area. Discuss theory
and research work which is relevant to the
research topic. Move from the general
area to the particular predictions to
be tested via a logical argument
showing why the predictions
have been made. Finally,
state the specific
hypothesis.

(Adapted from Coolican, 1990)

Given below is an example of an introduction that might be used for the practical we are undertaking.

INTRODUCTION

Many health care practitioners spend a considerable amount of time in giving information and advice to patients or clients about aspects of health care. Even so, lack of information remains a source of dissatisfaction for many patients and clients. Ley (1988) has summarised the findings from a large number of surveys and points out that approximately 30% of patients report dissatisfaction with the quality and amount of information they are given. This figure holds true for both hospitals and the community. Further, there is no indication of any improvement in the problem over the years.

Ley (1989) suggests that some of the dissatisfaction expressed rests on the fact that patients and clients do not remember the information they are given. A number of studies have shown that a considerable amount of advice and information is forgotten even when it is given to obtain informed consent to particular medical procedures. Cassileth *et al.* (1980) found, for example, that 200 cancer patients recalled on average 69% of the information that was offered to obtain their consent for treatment.

Although some of the forgetting may be due to anxiety and lack of familiarity with health care terminology, it is worth noting that a similar degree of information loss can be found in analogue studies undertaken with healthy volunteers (e.g. Ley, 1972). Research into human memory suggests some reasons why this might be the case. Postman and Phillips (1965) demonstrated that when there is a delay between hearing a list of words and recalling those words, recall of the early words is superior to recall of the later ones. This is known as a primacy effect. Ley and Spelman (1967) have reported a similar finding with recall of medical information. Some small-scale replications of Ley and Spelman's findings have been reported (e.g. Wattley and Müller, 1984) but using single words rather than statements. It seems worthwhile, therefore, to attempt to replicate the results using full statements giving health care information. It is expected that participants will be able to recall more initial statements giving health care information than later statements.

Can you see how this introduction funnels down from the general subject area through to a specific prediction? Each step in the argument is intended to follow from the one before so that the prediction emerges as a logical consequence of the literature that is considered. It is worth having a look at some more examples of introductions to research articles to see if you can trace the path from the general area to the specific prediction; there should be a clear and logical progression.

In the next session we will consider details of the procedure and you will be asked to test two participants.

Summary

1   Research questions can be derived from a variety of sources including the professional literature. It may be difficult, however, to make sense of a large research literature without some guidance from an experienced supervisor.

2   A series of steps need to be carried out in order to decide on an experimental design. These are to:

- identify the research question

- specify and vary the independent variable

- decide the size of the sample of participants and whether the same or different people are to experience the treatment conditions

- consider how to control any extraneous variables

- decide how to measure the effect of the experiment

- formulate the experimental hypothesis

- decide how the data will be analysed.

3   The introduction to an experimental report is the first section to be written. Its function is to provide a clear rationale for the study in the light of previous theory and evidence.

Before you move on to Session Three, check that you have achieved the objectives given at the beginning of this session, and, if not, review the appropriate sections.

Carrying out a small-scale experiment

Introduction

By the end of the last session we had decided on all the essential design features of the experiment which we will carry out. In other words, the basic structure of the study is in place, but some of the procedural details still need to be filled in. The aim of this session is to work out the remaining details, carry out the study and report what has been done in the method section of the report. You should note that you will need to find two people, preferably in the age range 25–42 years, who are prepared to take part in the experiment. They will each be needed for about 15 to 20 minutes, ideally one after the other. They should not have a medical or nursing background.

Session objectives

When you have completed this session, you should be able to:

- outline the kind of preparation required before undertaking an experiment

- describe what is required from the method section of a report of an experiment.

1: Working out the procedure

You may find it useful to think of designing an experiment as being rather like building a house. The first major step is to draw up all the details of the structure and to check carefully that the plans will work in practice. This is the process that we went through in the last session and we ended with a 'blueprint' for an experiment. We can now look at all the details and make minor adjustments where necessary. The essential structure should, however, remain untouched.

The first task, therefore, is to decide what details remain to be filled in. Use the following activity to see if you can identify where some finishing touches are needed.

ACTIVITY 12   ALLOW **10** MINUTES

Refer back to section 2 in Session Two. Can you think of any details of our proposed experiment that have not yet been decided? We have, for example, talked about a list of statements giving health care information but we have not, as yet, drawn up such a list.

Commentary

The list of details that I came up with are as follows:

- define the characteristics of the participants
- write a set of instructions to be used in order to standardise what participants are told
- define the experimental environment more closely
- decide on the number of statements to be presented
- write a list of statements to be used
- decide how to pace the presentation of the statements
- decide on the delay between presentation and recall
- decide how to record the findings
- decide how long to allow for recall
- decide what the participants should do between presentation and recall
- consider how accurate recall must be to be scored as correct.

We will, I suggest, find it easier to deal with each of these items if we divide them into participants, materials and procedure. Let's have a look at each in turn.

1 Participants

As was noted in Session Two, the majority of participants have been selected for you. There were 18 of them and they were all aged between 25 and 42 years. Four were male and the rest female. They were all students who volunteered to take part. None of them were taking health care courses and none had a nursing or medical background. You should try to match your participants as closely as possible to mine and check that the people you approach fall into the right age range and do not have a nursing or medical background.

2 Materials

The most important point under this heading is the list of health care statements to be used. Ley and Spelman (1967) found that using six, nine or 12 medical statements gave recall rates of 64 per cent, 53 per cent and 41 per cent respectively. Which do you think we should select? The danger is that if too few statements are used all of them will be remembered and so we will be unable to detect an effect of position. This is known as a **ceiling effect**. The danger of a **floor effect** is considerably less: even if the number of items are increased, people can usually still remember some of them. I suggest, therefore, that we use twelve items.

The actual items that I used with the 18 participants are:

1   You have a venous ulcer.
2   A zinc dressing has been used in the past.
3   A pinch skin graft might be helpful.
4   Do not worry if you cannot move around a great deal.
5   You should wear elastic stockings once the ulcer has healed.
6   The ulcer must be cleaned with a saline solution.
7   A district nurse is responsible for your care.
8   A four-layer bandage will be used in future.
9   Your foot may swell slightly because of the compression.
10   Your leg must be re-bandaged each week.
11   The compression exerted by the bandage will be measured at intervals.
12   Adhesive plaster will not be necessary.

As was noted in Session Two, the first six and the last six items need to be swapped for half of the subjects. The alternative order is therefore:

1   A district nurse is responsible for your care.
2   A four-layer bandage will be used in future.
3   Your foot may swell slightly because of the compression.
4   Your leg must be re-bandaged each week.
5   The compression exerted by the bandage will be measured at intervals.
6   Adhesive plaster will not be necessary.
7   You have a venous ulcer.
8   A zinc dressing has been used in the past.
9   A pinch skin graft might be helpful.
10   Do not worry if you cannot move around a great deal.
11   You should wear elastic stockings once the ulcer has healed.
12   The ulcer must be cleaned with a saline solution.

You will also need some paper and a biro for your participants to record the information that they can recall.

3   Procedure

I suggest that initially you tell the people you approach that you are carrying out a simple study of memory for health care information and that you need two people who are willing to take part; state that the study will take a maximum of twenty minutes, that the names of the individuals involved will not be recorded and, therefore, confidentiality and anonymity will be assured. This will give your participants a clear idea of what is going to happen in the study.

You will need a reasonably quiet and private room in which to carry out the study. The two people must be seen separately since they will receive different lists to recall. The precise instructions to be given to the participants are given below.

'I will read you a list of statements which might be made to a patient with a fairly common medical condition. There will then be a delay of ten minutes. Once the ten minutes are up, you will be asked to write down as many of the statements as you can recall in any order that you like. Do you have any questions?'

You should read the statements at a steady pace. Do not rush through and do not pause for long periods. You should practise first and should find that the list takes about 45 seconds to read. Try to fill the ten-minute delay by chatting with the

Ceiling effect: *this term is used when performance on a particular task is at a very high level. If this is the case, then improvements in performance cannot be produced by a treatment condition*

Floor effect: *this term is used when performance on a particular task is at a very low level. If this is the case, then reduction in performance cannot be produced by a treatment condition*

person that you are testing – you can get a cup of coffee if you have enough time. If you let your participants sit quietly, they may rehearse the items on the list and so improve their performance. At the end of the delay period, you should ask for recall of the items by saying,

'Please will you now write down as many of the statements as you can recall in any order that you like. You may not be able to recall the exact wording, but you should try to get as close to it as you can. You have five minutes.'

When each person has finished you should explain as fully as you can the purpose of the study and be prepared to answer any questions. It is worth stressing that the test is known to be difficult and that you did not expect all or most of the items to be recalled. This part of the study is known as **debriefing**; it is not a substitute for informed consent but it is used in addition to it. You can also get an interesting perspective by asking the participants about their view of the study.

Debriefing: *giving a full explanation of an experiment to people who have taken part*

When you come to look at the items recalled, I suggest that you are not too strict about what passes as correct. So, for example, for the item:

'The ulcer must be cleaned with a saline solution'

I accepted:
'The leg will be treated with saline'
'The ulcer may be washed with saltwater'

but not:
'The ulcer must be kept clean'
'Salt will be used'.

In the next section I shall give you a checklist of things that you need to do in order to complete your part of the practical exercise.

2: Collecting the results

The steps that you need to take can be divided into two parts. The first consists of some basic preparation.

ACTIVITY 13   ALLOW 30 MINUTES

Work your way through the check list given below.

1   Check back through this session and Session Two to be sure that you understand the details of the study so that you are able to explain it to your participants.

2   Make a clear copy of both sets of health care statements given above under the heading 'Materials' and of the instructions to be given to the participants.

3   Identify a quiet room that you can use.

4   Practise reading the statements at a reasonably slow and steady pace. Each list should take about 45 seconds in total.

5 Make sure that you have paper and a biro to be used for recall, and a watch to time the ten-minute delay period between presentation and recall as well as the five-minute recall period.

6 Find two people who meet the selection criteria and are willing to take part, and arrange a time for each of them.

Commentary

I realise that the preparation may seem to take rather a long time given that you will be collecting results from only two people. It is, nonetheless, well worth developing the habit of making careful and detailed preparations before you begin any piece of research.

The second part consists of the steps that you need to take in order to conduct the experiment.

ACTIVITY 14   ALLOW **60** MINUTES

For each of the participants, work your way through the checklist given below.

1 Read out the instructions to the participant and answer any questions.

2 Read out one of the list of statements. One list should be used for one person, and the alternative list for the other.

3 Remember to time the ten-minute delay period and to occupy the person while it passes.

4 When the ten minutes is up, give the participant paper and a biro and ask them to recall the statements. Remember to stop the participant when five minutes are up.

5 Offer to explain the study fully and to answer any questions. Ask the participants how the study felt from their point of view and record any comments.

6 Make a note of any ideas about the experiment that occur to you as you conduct it. Could you, for example, see any problems with the procedure that you have carried out?

7 Have a look at the recall and score the number of items remembered correctly.

8 Fasten together the list of items that you read with the list of items that were recalled and any comments or notes. This final point is crucial because, if you do not do it, you may lose track of which person heard which list and you will then be unable to sort out the results.

Commentary

I hope that you managed to do this without too many difficulties. I realise that it can be rather daunting to carry out this kind of study for the first time. This is a good time to write the method section of the report, since all of the details are still fresh in your mind. This aspect will be covered in more detail below.

3: Writing an experimental report - the method

Components of a method section

As was mentioned in Session Two, the method section of a report should include sufficient detail to allow the study to be replicated. This may be a rather laborious task, but it is absolutely essential. You may remember that in the paper by Holden, Sagovsky and Cox (1989) it was not easy to discover what care, if any, was offered to the control group. This omission made it somewhat difficult to interpret the findings that were presented. Did you find it irritating to have to hunt for the details in that paper?

Since it is all too easy to miss out some important details by accident, it is helpful to divide the method section into four sub-sections. They are:

- design
- participants
- materials
- procedure.

We used the last three of these sub-sections in planning the details of our experiment, and this was intended to help you to think about the kind of information that they should contain.

Design
This sub-section describes the structure or 'blueprint' of the experiment. It should outline the independent variable, the dependent variable, the treatment conditions, the kind of design used and any controls that have been employed.

Participants
The number and characteristics of people who took part in the study should be recorded here. You should also record how the sample was obtained.

Materials
Describe carefully any materials used in the experiment. If the materials are too lengthy to be described fully at this point, details can be included in an appendix and simply referred to here.

Procedure
In this section you should describe precisely the procedure that was used during the experiment. Any instructions given to participants should be included here or in an appendix.

The method
Given below is an example of a method section that might be used for the experiment we have just completed.

METHOD

Design
The independent variable was the position of items in the list and the dependent variable the number of items correctly recalled for each list position. Each participant was given a total score for the number of items correctly recalled from the first six and the last six list positions. The design can be regarded as repeated-measures with two treatment

conditions. The same list of items was used for all participants, but the list was divided into two halves and the set of items appearing first was counterbalanced across participants.

Participants

Eighteen people took part in the experiment (mean age 33 years; age range 25–42 years). Fourteen of the participants were female and four male. None had a background in either nursing or medicine. An **opportunity** or **convenience sample** was used.

Materials

A list of 12 health-care-related statements was used. These were as follows:

1　You have a venous ulcer.
2　A zinc dressing has been used in the past.
3　A pinch skin graft might be helpful.
4　Do not worry if you cannot move around a great deal.
5　You should wear elastic stockings once the ulcer has healed.
6　The ulcer must be cleaned with a saline solution.
7　A district nurse is responsible for your care.
8　A four-layer bandage will be used in future.
9　Your foot may swell slightly because of the compression.
10　Your leg must be re-bandaged each week.
11　The compression exerted by the bandage will be measured at intervals.
12　Adhesive plaster will not be necessary.

For the alternative list, items 7 to 12 became items 1 to 6 and items 1 to 6 became 7 to 12.

Procedure

Participants were tested individually in a quiet room. They were assigned randomly to one of the two list orders. The following instructions were read out.

'I will read you a list of statements which might be made to a patient with a fairly common medical condition. There will then be a delay of ten minutes. Once the ten minutes are up, you will be asked to write down as many of the statements as you can recall in any order that you like. Do you have any questions?'

The 12 statements were then read out at a steady pace, the entire sequence taking approximately 45 seconds. There was a ten-minute delay period before recall during which the participant was encouraged to talk in order to prevent rehearsal of the list items. Written recall was then requested as follows.

'Please will you now write down as many of the statements as you can recall in any order that you like. You may not be able to recall the exact wording, but you should try to get as close to it as you can. You have five minutes.'

At the end of the five minutes the paper was removed and the purpose of the experiment explained fully.

Opportunity/convenience sample: *a sample of people who fulfil particular selection criteria and are willing to take part in a study*

As you have seen, I have had to report the experiment using only 18 participants since this is the only data I have. Notice also that this section is written in the past tense as it describes a study that has been carried out. When you write a method section it is often helpful to give it to someone else to read. If they cannot extract all of the details easily, then this suggests that it needs to be revised.

Summary

1   Designing an experiment involves specifying the overall structure. When the design is complete, there are usually a number of procedural details that still need to be considered.

2   Preparing for and conducting experiments can take up a considerable amount of time – attention to detail is critical.

3   The method section of an experimental report should be written as soon after the results are collected as possible. It should provide sufficient detail to allow the experiment to be replicated.

Before you move on to Session Four, check that you have achieved the objectives given at the beginning of this session, and, if not, review the appropriate sections.

SESSION FOUR

Describing and analysing the results

Introduction

So far in this unit we have designed an experiment, specified the procedural details and collected the results. In this session we will take the next step, which is to use the findings we have gathered to test the experimental hypothesis. You have already encountered, in both Units One and Two, some of the concepts that you will need, so much of the material should be familiar. The aim of this session is, therefore, to integrate and extend your understanding of how to analyse and present numerical data.

Session objectives

When you have completed this session, you should be able to:

- organise and summarise the results of an experiment in order to illustrate the effect of changes in the independent variable

- explain the advantages of displaying results as a figure

- use the sign test to examine the significance of any differences between two sets of related scores

- describe the requirements of the results section of a report.

1: Describing the results

Organising the data

The results obtained from an experiment must be both described and analysed. The aim of the description is to provide a summary or summaries of the findings which show the overall pattern of the findings clearly; the aim of the analyses is to test the experimental hypothesis. The activities in this section will guide you through the process of describing and analysing the results from our experiment.

When you collect a set of results from an experiment, the first step is to organise the findings in some way. At the moment we have between us 20 separate sheets of paper each consisting of a list of items recalled by one of the participants. Before we can do anything else, each of those sheets must be scored and the scores collated in such a way that we will be able to go on to describe and analyse the findings.

By this time you should have examined and scored the results from your two participants. We will now look at that scoring and combine your scores with those that were obtained from the other 18 participants. The next activity will lead you through this operation.

ACTIVITY 15   ALLOW **10** MINUTES

You will have a set of items recalled by each of your participants. You should be able to match each recall list to the list of statements that was actually read out. You should now:

1   Check carefully your decision of 'correct' or 'incorrect' for each item recalled. If you are in doubt, try to find someone to discuss it with and reach a joint decision. Remember that recall does not need to be perfect, but the essential idea contained in the statement should have been recorded.

2   Complete the data sheet in *Table 1* for your two participants. Put '1' for each item correctly recalled and '0' for each item incorrectly recalled or omitted. The scores for 18 people have been provided for you.

List position		1	2	3	4	5	6	7	8	9	10	11	12
People	1	1	0	1	0	0	1	0	0	0	0	0	0
	2	1	1	1	0	0	0	0	0	0	0	1	0
	3	1	1	0	0	0	0	0	0	0	1	0	0
	4	1	0	1	1	0	0	0	0	0	0	0	1
	5	1	1	0	0	1	1	0	0	0	0	1	0
	6	1	1	0	1	0	0	0	0	0	0	0	0
	7	0	0	1	1	1	0	0	0	0	0	0	1
	8	1	1	1	0	0	0	0	0	0	0	0	0
	9	1	0	1	0	0	1	0	0	0	0	0	0
	10	1	1	0	1	0	1	0	0	0	0	0	0
	11	0	0	1	1	1	0	0	0	0	0	0	1
	12	1	0	1	1	0	0	0	0	0	0	1	0
	13	1	0	1	0	0	1	0	1	0	0	0	1
	14	1	1	0	1	0	0	0	0	0	1	0	1
	15	1	1	1	0	0	0	0	0	0	0	1	0
	16	1	0	1	1	0	0	0	0	0	0	1	0
	17	1	1	0	1	0	0	0	0	0	0	0	0
	18	0	1	1	0	0	1	0	1	0	1	0	1
	19												
	20												

Table 1 Individual scores

Commentary

Although organising the data in this way is a necessary step, it tells us relatively little about the pattern of the results that have been obtained. This table contains what are known as **raw data**; that is to say, scores that have not been summarised or analysed in any way.

Raw data: *the actual scores that have been obtained from individuals taking part in a study*

Summarising the data

Our next step is to summarise these raw data so as to show the pattern of the results we have obtained. In any experiment the focus of interest is the effects of the independent variable; that is, we want to know whether or not changes in the independent variable have produced differences in the results for each of the treatment conditions. This being the case, the most usual approach is to begin by averaging the data obtained for each treatment condition. The activity below will help you to carry out this process for our data.

ACTIVITY 16 ALLOW **10** MINUTES

Follow the steps listed below to produce a summary of the data we have obtained.

1   Using the raw data that I obtained, I have totalled the scores from each of the 18 participants for list conditions 1–6 and 7–12 separately. Carry out the same operation for your two participants and write your totals in the spaces in *Table 2*.

List position		1–6	7–12
People	1	3	0
	2	3	1
	3	2	1
	4	3	1
	5	4	1
	6	3	0
	7	3	1
	8	3	0
	9	3	0
	10	4	0
	11	3	1
	12	3	1
	13	3	2
	14	3	2
	15	3	1
	16	3	1
	17	3	0
	18	3	3
	19		
	20		

Table 2 Individual scores for each condition

<table>
<tr><td>

To Calculate a Mean

1 Add up all the scores.

2 Divide the result by the total number of scores:

e.g. $5 + 10 + 6 = 21$

$$Mean = \frac{21}{3} = 7$$

</td></tr>
</table>

2 Now calculate the means for the first six positions and the last six positions separately and add them to *Table 3*. You do this by adding the scores for each column and dividing by the total number, in this case, 20. The means for my 18 individuals have been entered in brackets as an example.

List position	Mean items recalled
1–6	(2.8)
7–12	(0.8)

Table 3 Means of scores for first six and last six list positions

3 Because the mean gives no indication of the spread of scores, we also need to find the range of scores for each of the two treatment conditions. You do this by finding the highest score in each of the two columns and subtracting from it the lowest score for the same column. Fill in the two ranges in *Table 4*. The ranges from the 18 participants have been given in brackets.

List position	Mean items recalled	Range
1–6	(2.8)	(2)
7–12	(0.8)	(3)

Table 4 Means and ranges of scores for each condition

Commentary

You may have wondered why we are using a mean rather than a total to summarise the results for each treatment condition. It is simply because the total would not reflect the magnitude of a score obtained by any individual. The mean or any other **measure of central tendency** is used to provide a single score which is representative of a set of scores (see Clegg, 1982, pp. 13–23; Greene, 1990, pp. 42–43; Caulcott, 1992, pp. 47–64).

Did you understand why we calculated the range as well as the mean? A **measure of dispersion,** such as the range, is included to give an idea of the spread or scatter of the scores (see Clegg, pp. 24–30; Caulcott, pp. 65–73). Without this information the mean can be rather misleading.

Measures of central tendency and measures of dispersion are the two categories of **descriptive statistics.** The aim of descriptive statistics is to describe sets of numbers briefly and accurately. The purpose of using them to describe the scores obtained in an experiment is to demonstrate the pattern of results. In other words, descriptive statistics are used to have an initial look at the effects of changes in the independent variable on the scores obtained in each treatment condition.

Presenting the data

The summary that we produced at the end of Activity 16 can be included as a **table** in the results section of the experimental report. In many cases a table can be translated fairly directly into a **line graph** or **bar chart** to provide a **figure.** In our experiment, since we have data for each of the 12 list positions, we can produce a more informative figure by using the data for each of the positions rather than averages of the first six and the last six. We will now work briefly through the steps needed to produce a suitable figure using the data from the 18 individuals.

To obtain the data we need we will have to go back to *Table 1* and total the scores for each list position. These data are given in *Table 5*, along with the percentage of items recalled correctly, since this makes it easier for a reader to understand changes in performance across positions.

To calculate the percentages:

1   Divide a score by the maximum possible score.
2   Multiply the result by 100:

e.g. Maximum possible score for list position 1 with 18 participants = 18

Total correct score for list position 1 with 18 participants = 15
$$\frac{15}{18} = 0.83$$
Percentage = 0.83 x 100 = 83%

List position	My totals	Percentage recalled
1	15	83%
2	10	56%
3	12	67%
4	9	50%
5	3	17%
6	7	39%
7	0	0%
8	2	11%
9	0	0%
10	3	17%
11	5	28%
12	6	33%

Table 5 Totals and percentages of scores for each list position

Measure of central tendency: *a single score which is intended to be representative of a set of scores*

Measure of dispersion: *a single score which is intended to show the spread or scatter of a set of scores*

Descriptive statistics: *the two scores (one of central tendency and the other of dispersion) which are used to characterise a set of scores*

Table: *a data summary presented as a set of numbers*

Line graph: *a graphical representation of data which is used when the independent variable varies in quantity or amount*

Bar chart: *a graphical representation of data which is used when the independent variable varies in type or presence/absence*

Figure: *a data summary in which a set of numbers have been converted into a graphical form*

Horizontal axis: *the line at the bottom of a graph which is used to represent the independent variable*

Vertical axis: *the line on a graph perpendicular to the horizontal axis which is used to represent the dependent variable*

On a line graph the independent variable is normally represented on the **horizontal axis** and the dependent variable on the **vertical axis.** The graph that I plotted using the data in *Table 5* is shown in *Figure 1*.

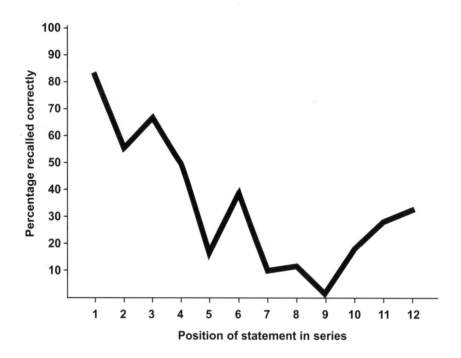

Figure 1 Percentage of items recalled correctly by list position

When the curve is plotted in this way it does not look very smooth. Can you see how we might give a clearer impression of the results? We could average the results for pairs of list positions which would make the effect more obvious. Let's see what this would look like.

ACTIVITY 17   ALLOW **15** MINUTES

Average the percentages for pairs of list conditions from all 20 subjects and then plot a graph similar to the one in *Figure 1*. This will give you six rather than twelve points along the horizontal axis.

Commentary

Serial position curve: *a graph showing correct recall of items against the serial position of items in a list*

You should now have a graph which shows the primacy effect very clearly: statements which appeared early in the list were more likely to be recalled than statements which appeared later. The curve which we have plotted to show the effect is known in research on human memory as a **serial position curve**. Can you see the advantages of showing the data in graphical as well as in tabular form? Figures have more immediate impact than tables and allow trends or relationships in the data to be understood more readily.

Both tables and graphs can be included in the results section of an experimental report. If they are, they must be numbered and given a title. The title should state precisely what the table or figure contains. So, for example, the graph that you have just plotted could be labelled in this way:

Figure 1: Percentage of items correctly recalled for pairs of list positions

The next step is to move away from description to look at using the data to test the experimental hypothesis; this will be tackled in the following section.

2: Analysing the results

In Session Two of this unit we produced an experimental hypothesis for this study. It was:

'Participants will be able to recall more initial statements giving health care information than later statements.'

We now have to test this hypothesis in order to establish if the results from the experiment support it or not. Even though the difference between initial and later statements looks fairly clear, it is necessary to obtain an estimate of the likelihood, or probability, of that pattern of results occurring by chance alone.

Statistical tests

In Unit One, Session Five, some of the essential principles behind statistical testing were described; you may like to have a look back to that session now to remind yourself of the ideas. It was noted that statistical tests can be used to examine the differences between sets of scores. The aim is to disentangle the experimental effect we are after from random error. In other words, we want to establish as far as possible whether any observed differences are due:

- entirely to random error

or

- at least in part, to some constant effect (either the independent variable or a confounding variable).

In order to meet this aim, the relevant statistical tests make use of different kinds of information. Put simply, these are:

- the number of participants

- the magnitude of the difference between treatment conditions

- the dispersion of scores within treatment conditions.

The last item in this list gives you a clue as to the first step you have to take in order to carry out a statistical test. You need to assemble the data in such a way that it includes a score or scores for each individual taking part in the study. We will work through all the steps you need to take using the data from our experiment as an example.

1 Assemble the data

Data must be assembled in such a way that there is a score or scores for each individual who completed the study. We have done this already in *Table 2* on p. 38. Have a look back to that table now.

You will notice that we have produced the scores for each individual by totalling across six different list positions. Since statistical tests make use of the dispersion of scores from different individuals in the same treatment condition, you must not add scores from different individuals together before carrying out a statistical test.

2 Select an appropriate test

The question of how to select an appropriate statistical test is not one that can be dealt with here in full. You should have a look through one of the recommended statistics books if you need to. You will find that the rules are fairly straightforward. Clegg (1982) and Greene (1990) are both particularly clear on how to select an appropriate test; the latter also has a useful decision chart for this purpose. Most of the basic statistical texts also include clear and simple instructions for how to carry out a range of different tests.

Related: *a term used to describe scores in different treatment conditions which are produced by the same or matched individuals*

In this study we are going to use one of the simplest statistical tests which is known as the sign test. The sign test can be used to examine the significance of any differences between two sets of **related** scores. It cannot be used with **unrelated** scores. Working through this test should help to reassure you that the procedure can be very simple and does not require any complex knowledge of mathematics!

3 Carry out the test

Unrelated: *a term used to describe scores in different treatment conditions which are produced by different individuals*

STEP 1: Subtract each score in one column from its partner in the other column. Record the sign of the difference, either plus or minus. This operation has been carried out for our scores and the result is shown in *Table 6*.

List position	1–6	7–12	Step 1
People 1	3	0	+3
2	3	1	+2
3	2	1	+1
4	3	1	+2
5	4	1	+3
6	3	0	+3
7	3	1	+2
8	3	0	+3
9	3	0	+3
10	4	0	+4
11	3	1	+2
12	3	1	+2
13	3	2	+1
14	3	2	+1
15	3	1	+2
16	3	1	+2
17	3	0	+3
18	3	3	0

Table 6 Step 1 of the sign test

STEP 2: Count up the number of pluses and minuses. Ignore any zeroes. So:

+ = 17
− = 0

STEP 3: Select the smaller of those two values and call it 'S'. Count the total number of pluses and minuses and call it 'N'. So:

S = 0
N = 17

(Adapted from Clegg, 1982)

Significance

The next step is to use our value of 'S' to find out the likelihood of the differences between the conditions occurring entirely due to random error or to the effects of chance alone. But in order for you to consult a statistical table and make use of the information in it, you will need to have a more precise understanding of the notion of significance. Resource 1 should give you a grasp of the essential ideas.

ACTIVITY 18   ALLOW 30 MINUTES

Work your way through Resource 1 entitled 'There are lies, damned lies and statistics' which is taken from *Research Awareness, Module 9: The Experimental Perspective* (Clark, 1988). You will find it helpful to carry out the activities which are included. You have encountered many of the basic concepts in this unit and the previous one and so some of the material will be familiar. Once you have read it, note down answers to the following questions about our experiment.

1 What is the general term for the kind of statistics that we have been carrying out in this section?

2 What significance level do you think we should be using?

3 Is our experimental hypothesis one-tailed or two-tailed?

Commentary

1 We have been carrying out **inferential statistics** in this section.

2 The standard significance level is 0.05 and this the highest level of probability that we would accept as statistically significant. As Clark points out, we should ideally have set the significance level at the outset.

3 Our experimental hypothesis is one-tailed since we predicted that initial statements would be recalled more readily than later ones.

Inferential statistics: *statistical tests which allow inferences about a population to be drawn from observations made on a sample*

You can now make use of all of the understanding that you have acquired to consult the statistical table for the sign test.

STEP 4: Consult a table of values for S which gives you the probability that the difference between the conditions is due to chance alone. This is included as *Table 7*.

In our example we have calculated that N=17. Look down the left-hand column under N until you find the appropriate line. Now proceed across the columns comparing each value that you encounter to our value of S. If our value of S is less than the table value, then move on to the next column. You will find that our value of S (which is 0) is less than the value of 1 given in the extreme right-hand column.

To discover the level of significance, you will need to look at the figures given in the very top row – remember that the experimental hypothesis and therefore the test are one-tailed. Because our value of S is less than 1, we can say that our result is significant beyond the 0.0005 level. This result can be written as $p < 0.0005$. That is, there is a probability of less than 0.05 in 100 that the results have arisen by chance alone. We can, therefore, reject the null hypothesis that the observed difference is due entirely to random error.

N	Level of significance for one-tailed test				
	0.05	0.025	0.01	0.005	0.0005
	Level of significance for two-tailed test				
	0.10	0.05	0.02	0.01	0.001
5	0	–	–	–	–
6	0	0	–	–	–
7	0	0	0	–	–
8	1	0	0	0	–
9	1	1	0	0	–
10	1	1	0	0	–
11	2	1	1	0	0
12	2	2	1	1	0
13	3	2	1	1	0
14	3	2	2	1	0
15	3	3	2	2	1
16	4	3	2	2	1
17	4	4	3	2	1
18	5	4	3	3	1
19	5	4	4	3	2
20	5	5	4	3	2
25	7	7	6	5	4
30	10	9	8	7	5
35	12	11	10	9	7

Table 7 Critical values of S

What can be said about the experimental hypothesis? The results of the statistical test support the experimental hypothesis, although it has not been proved or established beyond any shadow of doubt. Further, even though we can now accept that the observed difference is unlikely to be due to chance, we still have not isolated the actual cause of the difference. The fact that the experimental hypothesis is supported, does not mean that the independent variable is necessarily responsible.

We have now described and analysed our data sufficiently to write the results section of the report. The work you have just done should have given you a basic grasp of the principles and applications of inferential statistics.

3: Writing a results section

Think back to Session Two where we considered the purpose of the results section, which, it was noted, should report any analyses of the data but should not include any interpretation of them. Given below is a results section that might be written for the experiment we carried out. The data from 18 participants have been used.

RESULTS

As shown in *Table 1*, there was a clear tendency for the first items in the list to be recalled more accurately than later items. The raw data are included in Appendix 1.

List position	Mean items recalled	Range
1–6	2.8	2
7–12	0.8	3

Table 1: Mean number of items recalled and ranges from early and late list positions

The percentage of items correctly recalled was plotted for pairs of list positions, as shown in *Figure 1*. Correct recall decreased from approximately 70% for list positions 1 and 2 to 28% for positions 5 and 6, demonstrating a clear primacy effect.

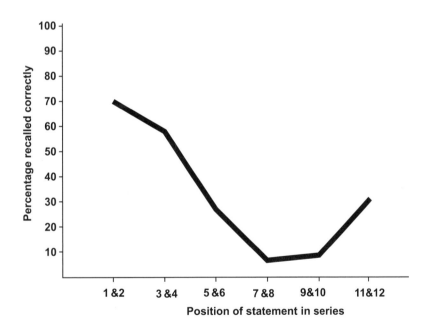

Figure 1 Percentage of items correctly recalled for pairs of list positions

The data were analysed further by comparing the total scores of individuals for the first six and the last six items. A sign test was employed and the difference was found to be highly significant at the 0.0005 level (S=0; N=17; sign test; one-tailed hypothesis). The calculations for the test are included in Appendix 2.

There are two points that you should note about this section. First, it is stated that the raw data and the statistical calculations are included in appendices. This is usual for practical reports but not for published articles. The purpose is to allow the person who is marking the practical to check that the data summaries and data analyses are both appropriate and accurate.

Second, both the figures and the tables have been numbered and given a title. Unless this is done, you cannot refer to them clearly in the text, and the reader may not be able to sort out what their contents are meant to be.

Finally, I should like to emphasise a very important point. When this study was planned, data analysis was mentioned but not discussed in any detail. The omission occurred because we were not ready to explore statistical tests at that point. Under normal circumstances, you must decide precisely how the data are to be analysed before you start the experiment. It is perfectly possible to design, plan and carry out an experiment only to realise that the data cannot be analysed statistically in any way at all. Do please make sure that this does not happen to you.

In the next session, we shall go on to look at how to interpret our findings.

Summary

1   Sets of scores can be summarised using descriptive statistics. These are a measure of central tendency and a measure of dispersion. In an experiment, the aim is to show the effects of changes in the independent variable on scores obtained in the different treatment conditions.

2   Inferential statistics can be used to estimate the probability that any differences between treatment conditions are due to chance alone. A basic test can be carried out by following a series of steps.

3   Decisions about which statistical test or tests to use to analyse the raw data should be regarded as an integral part of designing an experiment and be made before the data are collected.

4   The results section of a report of an experiment should describe any analyses of the data but should not include any interpretation of the analyses.

Before you move on to Session Five, check that you have achieved the objectives given at the beginning of this session, and, if not, review the appropriate sections.

Drawing conclusions from the results

Introduction

As we have already discussed, the overall aim of experimental research is to provide answers to predictive research questions. Having carried out a small-scale experiment and collected the data, the relationship between the results and the research question must be systematically addressed. In essence this is the function of a discussion section of a research report. In this session you will be guided through the points that you need to consider in order to draw conclusions from experimental results and so write a clear and informative discussion.

Session objectives

When you have completed this session, you should be able to:

- explain the elements involved in the interpretation of an experiment

- describe the requirements of the discussion section of an experimental report.

1: Interpreting experimental results

The aim of interpretation

In the previous session we discussed how to summarise, analyse and present the findings from our experiment. The pattern of results we obtained looked extremely clear; even so, the findings need to be interpreted. Why, given that the results seem to be obvious, do we need to do anything further? I recently asked a similar question of a group of health care students. Their initial reaction was that the aim of the interpretation was to translate 'numbers into words' in order to make the findings totally clear. If this were the case, then the 'interpretation' of our experiment would merely consist of the following statement:

'In this experiment it was found that the recall of statements from the first six list positions was significantly different from the recall of statements from the last six list positions.'

Is this satisfactory? When looked at in this way, it seems clear that simply translating 'numbers into words' provides a redescription of the findings rather than an interpretation. Interpreting the findings of an experiment involves deciding what those findings actually mean. In other words, in order to draw conclusions from the findings you need to go well beyond the information contained in the results section of the report. Use the following activity to think about the kinds of thing that need to be taken into account when interpreting the results of an experiment.

ACTIVITY 19　　　　　ALLOW **10** MINUTES

Think back to the experiment we have just completed. Make a list of what you would need to take into account in order to interpret the findings of that experiment. Most, but not necessarily all, of what you need should be contained in sections of the report that have already been written. Would you, for example, want to relate our results to details of the procedure?

Commentary

When a similar exercise was carried out with a group of health care students, a considerable number of possible items were collected. The list consisted of:

- a summary of the findings
- the results of any analyses carried out on the data
- the research question
- the experimental hypothesis
- details of the experimental design
- details of the experimental procedure
- previous related research
- previous theoretical accounts
- new theoretical explanations.

Your list may have contained most of these items or you may have concentrated mainly on the method and procedure of the experiment.

Elements involved in interpretation

Clearly, the interpretation of an experiment involves a number of different elements. Let's look at these now.

1   The summaries of the data and the results of the statistical tests given in the results section do need to be interpreted as well as redescribed. This involves considering details such as the direction of any differences between the treatment conditions and the magnitude of those differences. Further, you need to think about distinctive features of the data such as a wide range of scores in one or more of the conditions. In other words, only by a very careful inspection of the data can you begin to think about what those findings might mean. Such an examination moves beyond the calculation of descriptive or inferential statistics. In our study, for example, it was noticeable that nearly all the participants found the early items easier to recall than the later ones.

2   The results need to be set clearly into the context of the experimental hypothesis and the research question. One element of interpretation must be to match what was actually found against the predictions that were made at the start. If the experimental hypothesis was clearly and precisely stated, then it should be relatively easy to decide whether the results of the statistical tests support it or not. Since the experimental hypothesis is derived from the original research question, you would now have a partial answer to that question. I use the word 'partial' because, as has been emphasised, the experimental hypothesis may be accepted or rejected statistically for reasons other than the effects of the independent variable. If, for example, we had only used one version of the list and the early items had been more memorable than the later ones, then the experimental hypothesis would have been supported but an alternative explanation would exist for the results.

3   This brings us onto the third element of the interpretation. That is, you need to scrutinise the design and the procedure of the experiment with extreme care in order to identify any factors, other than the independent variable, which may have affected the results. If either the internal validity or the sensitivity of the experiment is in doubt, then any statistical test of the experimental hypothesis will not provide an unambiguous answer to the research question. So, for example, use of a relatively small sample may reduce the sensitivity of an experiment and allow the effects of the independent variable to be obscured. Further, you must also consider the extent to which you can safely generalise the findings. Even if your experiment is internally valid, it may nonetheless lack external validity and the findings may only hold true for a particular group of participants in a particular setting at a given time. We might, for instance, have established that order of presentation affects recall of health care information, but not be able to guarantee that the same effect would occur in older people, or in clinical settings.

4   You need to interpret the findings from your experiment in the light of previous relevant research and theorising. You should consider if the findings conflict or agree with previous results and search for reasons for any conflict. If your experimental hypothesis was intended to test a particular theory, then the implications of the results for that theory should be discussed.

We have separated out four elements which are involved in the interpretation of an experiment. It is only when you have considered each of those elements that you can finally draw conclusions from the results. The meaning of experimental findings depends, therefore, not only on the research question with which you started, but also upon all the decisions which you made in the course of designing, planning and carrying out the study and analysing the data. To put it another way, the goal of interpreting an experiment is to draw conclusions from the findings; the process of interpretation involves a consideration of all those details which might affect the legitimacy and generality of the conclusions.

Although we have identified a number of separate elements involved in the interpretation of an experiment, we have not considered the order in which to approach them or how the various elements fit together. So, the next task is to consider the process of interpretation in a little more detail.

Self-assessment question

6   Decide which of the following statements are true or false:

(a)   The sole aim of interpreting an experiment is to provide an answer to the research question.

(b)   If an experimental hypothesis is rejected then it can be concluded that the independent variable has no effect.

(c)   If an experiment lacks internal validity it may still be externally valid.

(d)   If an experiment lacks sensitivity and no significant difference is found, then the possibility of a causal relationship between the independent variable and the dependent variable still remains.

2: The process of interpretation

There are no strict rules or regulations for carrying out the process of interpretation, and different researchers approach the task in different ways. The method which I will outline reflects my own preferences, but you might like to talk to other researchers to find out their views.

In order to make all the points clear, we shall work through the process of interpreting an experiment. We will begin by looking at the kind of conclusions that might be drawn and then at the details which might cause you to modify or qualify those conclusions. We will then go on to consider the overall implications of the conclusions that have been drawn.

The fate of the experimental hypothesis

As has been emphasised, the starting point of any piece of experimental research is a predictive research question – regardless of the source from which that question was derived. The primary reason for carrying out the experiment is to provide an answer to the question. In the process of designing an experiment the research question is, however, translated into an experimental hypothesis. A logical place to start the interpretation, therefore, is by examining the fate of the experimental hypothesis. In order to do this, the important aspects of the data summaries and analyses need to be considered. So, diagrammatically, the process so far looks like this:

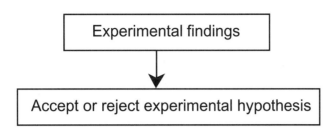

Figure 2 The process of interpretation, Stage 1

A preliminary answer to the research question

In our study, for example, the experimental hypothesis was clearly supported. As we noted above, however, the fate of the experimental hypothesis provides only a partial answer to the research question. Even though that answer may need to be qualified or modified later, it is worth being clear what the findings seem at first glance to imply for the research question. If the research question related to previous findings or theories, then any agreements or discrepancies between previous and current findings should be considered, and the possible consequences for any theory noted. Our results, for example, fitted well with Ley and Spelman (1967) and suggested that some of the problems which patients have in retaining information are not only due to stress or anxiety. Thus:

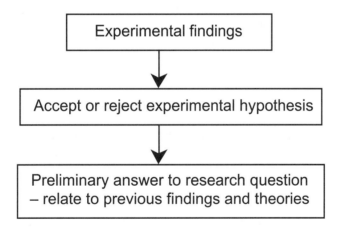

Figure 3 The process of interpretation, Stage 2

Internal validity and sensitivity

It is now essential to consider any features of the design or procedure which may force you to modify or limit your conclusions. If a significant difference has been obtained between the treatment conditions, then the search will focus on possible confounding variables which would provide alternative explanations. Can you think of any possibilities in our study?

If there are no significant differences, then you would look carefully at the sensitivity of the design and the data analyses to be sure that they were capable of detecting the effects of the independent variable. If this had been the case in our study, we would have noted the small sample size. So, the process can be extended in the following way:

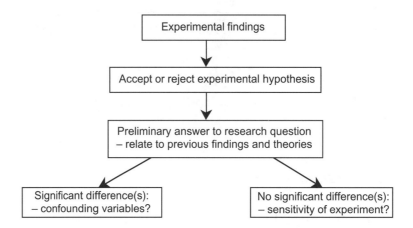

Figure 4 The process of interpretation, Stage 3

It is worth emphasising that the features of the experiment you should examine with care are those which will help you to interpret the findings that have been obtained. In other words, the relevance of features of the design, procedure and analyses depends critically on the nature of the results. The following activity should help to illustrate this important point.

ACTIVITY 20　　　　　　ALLOW 5 MINUTES

In our experiment, we found a highly significant difference in the recall of items from the different list positions. Early items were recalled considerably better than later ones. Now look at the list of details given below and note which ones might be relevant to an interpretation of our results:

- the experimental room was noisy for all participants

- the experimental room was noisy for some participants

- the experimental room tended to be noisy in the middle portion of the list

- the list items were not all equally difficult to recall

- the items at the start of the lists may have been easier to recall.

Commentary

Given that we obtained a significant difference between the conditions, we would be interested in details which might serve as alternative explanations of that result. In the list above, the only possible candidates are:

- the experimental room tended to be noisy in the middle portion of the list
- the items at the start of the lists may have been easier to recall.

All of the other details may be true, but they cannot be offered as alternative explanations of the findings. This exercise should have helped you to appreciate that features of the design, procedure and analyses are only relevant in the context of the actual results.

A modified answer to the research question

Having examined as many relevant details as you can think of, you are now in a position to modify or qualify the preliminary answer to the research question accordingly. You can now comment on the relationship between the independent and dependent variables demonstrated within the experiment. So:

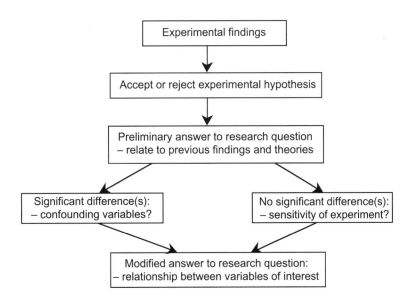

Figure 5 The process of interpretation, Stage 4

External validity and implications

You can now begin to try to set the experiment in a wider context. You should consider any factors which limit the generalisability of the findings such as the situation in which the experiment was performed, the materials that were used and the people who took part. You may also want to offer a theoretical explanation of the findings which may help to generate further research, or propose further studies that could be carried out. For example, we might want to know if forgetting of later items by patients occurs even when very important information is given at the end.

Although the potential applications of the findings to professional practice might not strictly be a part of the interpretation of experimental results, they could also be considered at this point. Our findings suggest that health care practitioners need to be aware of how much and which information people are likely to forget. So, to finish off our diagram:

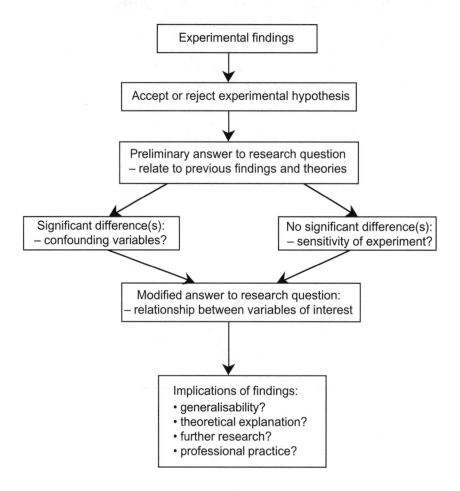

Figure 6 The process of interpretation, Stage 5

In practice, you may well find that this way of organising the interpretation of an experiment does not suit you or does not suit the particular study that you have carried out. Whatever approach you take, the aim in the end is to provide the clearest interpretation that you can and to be able to present that interpretation in a logical sequence in the discussion section of a report. In the next section we shall look at how to write a discussion.

3: Writing a research report - the discussion

Students sometimes find the discussion section of a research report the most challenging part to write. I have often been asked if some of the information from the introduction should be reserved to 'fill up the discussion'. This has the unfortunate effect of turning the discussion into a general essay on the topic with which the experiment is concerned. Rather, the aim of a discussion should be to interpret and explain the findings in the light of relevant information drawn from all of the preceding sections of the report.

Below you will find a discussion of the experiment we carried out using the overall plan for interpretation that was discussed above. As you read through it, note how the plan has been put into operation.

DISCUSSION

In this study, nearly all the participants recalled more items from the beginning of the list than from the end. On average, approximately three out of the first six items were recalled accurately but only one out of the last six. The superior recall of early items can be seen clearly in *Figure 1* and a highly significant difference was found in recall scores for early and late list positions.

These findings provide clear support for the experimental hypothesis and suggest that the order of presentation of statements intended to convey health care information has a marked effect on memory for those statements. The primacy effect that was obtained is very similar to that demonstrated by Ley and Spelman (1967) and Wattley and Müller (1984). Clearly, recall of medical information is far from perfect in healthy volunteers. This suggests that the forgetting which has often been recorded in patients in clinical situations may be due to problems of human memory as well as to anxiety and stress.

Although full statements rather than single medical terms were deliberately chosen for use in this experiment, the choice did present some drawbacks. Because the statements were intended to represent those that might be made to a patient by a practitioner, the order of the statements had to be logical. Ideally, the order of presentation should have been randomised. This would have served to guard against the possibility that more memorable items appeared at the start of the list and more difficult items at the end. Because only two orders of presentation were used, the ease of recall of items may have been partly or wholly responsible for the findings obtained. The study should, therefore, be replicated using different materials.

Even so, the considerable accord between this study and other studies suggests that the findings are due, at least in part, to the order in which the items were presented. The use of healthy volunteers and a fairly restricted age range may, however, restrict the extent to which the findings can be generalised. Older people may, for example, have different or additional difficulties with both the storage and retrieval of medical information.

Furthermore, in analogue studies such as this, volunteers are asked to recall information which is not personally relevant for them. Nonetheless, as Ley (1988) points out there is a remarkable similarity between the success with which real patients remember what they are told and the recall of volunteers in analogue studies both in the amount recalled and in the presence of primacy effects.

Overall, this study seems to confirm the idea that a considerable amount of information offered to patients will not be retained. Moreover, if early information is recalled best, then there is no guarantee that the most important items will be the ones that are remembered. Even though the forgetting may reflect a basic feature of human memory, it is likely that the problem is made worse by lack of familiarity with medical terminology. Ley (1989) suggests that memory, understanding, satisfaction and compliance are all strongly interrelated. It seems important, therefore, for health care practitioners to be aware of the potential problems and to try to ensure that information given is both understood and remembered.

There are two further points which you should note about the discussion section. First, the past tense is used when referring to the findings of the experiment. This is because, unlike the introduction, the discussion examines a study that has been carried out. Second, it is important to note that all the issues that were raised in the introduction have been mentioned or discussed in the discussion. If a point is sufficiently important to be included in the introduction, then it must be addressed further in the light of the findings of the experiment.

In the next session we shall put all of the sections of the report together and check that they form an integrated and coherent report.

Self-assessment questions

7   We have now completed the introduction, method, results and discussion sections of our report. What is still missing?

8   Can findings from other related studies help to confirm:

●   the internal validity

and/or

●   the external validity of a study which you are trying to interpret?

Give reasons for your answer.

Summary

1   The interpretation of findings from an experiment involves relating the results to the aims and method of the study.

2   The discussion section of an experimental report should guide the reader through the process of interpretation and state the conclusions that can reasonably be drawn.

Before you move on to Session Six, check that you have achieved the objectives given at the beginning of this session, and, if not, review the appropriate sections.

SESSION SIX

Presenting a research report

Introduction

In this session we will bring together all the sections of the report that we have written so far and add the title and the abstract. We will also draw up a checklist to help you to ensure that you have included all the necessary details. Overall, the aim of the session is to help you to examine your own work as critically as you have examined experimental reports presented by other people. The skills of designing, carrying out and reporting experimental research and the skills of evaluation, rather than being distinct from each other, can be seen as overlapping and complementary.

Session objectives

When you have completed this session, you should be able to:

● describe all the components of an experimental report

● discuss the style required in writing an experimental report.

1: Writing a research report - the title and references

We now need to put the finishing touches to our report in the form of the title, abstract and list of references. We will consider each of these in turn.

The title

In Session Two we noted that the title of a research report should indicate precisely the topic that is being investigated. For an experiment it is often sufficient to use the form, 'The effects of (independent variable) on (dependent variable)'. Have a try at writing the title for our experiment.

ACTIVITY 21　　　ALLOW 10 MINUTES

Using the form given above, write a title for our experiment. Then read through the list of titles from reports of experimental research given below. Try to decide the reasons for any variations in the basic form that you can see.

'The effect of living alone on bereavement symptoms'

'Umbilical cord clamping and pre-term infants: a randomised trial'

'Effects of touch in patients during a crisis situation in hospital'

'Sex and status: a study of the effects of gender and occupation on nurses' evaluation of nursing research'

'Ultrasound and pulsed electromagnetic energy treatment for perineal trauma. A randomised placebo-controlled trial'

'Twelve-hour shifts for nursing staff: a field experiment'

Commentary

The title I arrived at is: 'The effects of order of presentation on recall of statements conveying health care information'. Yours may have been fairly similar.

As you can see from the small selection provided, you often find titles in the form that has been outlined. The form is usually varied when the author wants to draw attention to an important or unusual feature of the study or of the findings. So 'field experiment' or 'randomised controlled trial' may well be mentioned.

The references

The references section of a report should consist of a complete list of sources; it is important to include *all* the items to which you have referred. In published articles the specific format used can vary from journal to journal according to the conventions that are adopted. If you are interested, you will find that Moorbath (1988) gives an excellent brief guide to the different systems used for citing references.

Although the choice of convention is not important, what is crucial is that you use one style consistently. A well-used one that you might like to adopt is known as the Harvard system of referencing, which is the system used in these Units. In the body of the text, sources are referred to by giving the surname of the author (or authors) followed by the date of publication in brackets. Then, in the reference section, all sources are given in alphabetical order. Journal articles are listed in the following form:

Dawes, M., Green, J. and Ashurst, H. (1992) 'Routine weighing in pregnancy', *British Medical Journal*, 304, pp. 487–489.

Books are referenced like this:

Hyland, M. and Donaldson, M. (1989) *Psychological Care in Nursing Practice,* Scutari Press.

And articles or chapters from books like this:

Chalmers, I., Enkin, M. and Keirse, M. (1989) 'Effective care in pregnancy and childbirth: a synopsis for guiding research and practice', in Chalmers, I., Enkin, M. and Keirse, M. (eds) *Effective Care in Pregnancy and Childbirth,* Oxford University Press.

When you are quoting the results of a study from a textbook rather than from the original article, you should use the following format (which is generally not used in published papers but it is for practical reports):

'Goldstein (1957), as cited in . . .'

Although we have added both the title and the references at the end of our work on the report, it is important to compile the reference list as you write the report. If you do not do this, you may lose track of a particular reference and be unable to rediscover it. The abstract, by contrast, should always be written when the rest of the report is complete. In the next section, we will look at the full report and write an appropriate abstract.

2: Writing a research report – the abstract and the style

The full report

Since the purpose of an abstract is to provide a succinct and accurate summary of what was done, what was found and any conclusions that were drawn, it can only be written when the full report is either in your head or on paper in front of you. I will bring together all the different sections of the report below, adding the references and appendices as well, and then ask you to have a go at writing an abstract.

The effects of order of presentation on recall of statements conveying health care information

INTRODUCTION

Many health care practitioners spend a considerable amount of time giving information and advice to patients or clients about aspects of health care. Even so, lack of information remains a source of dissatisfaction for many patients and clients. Ley (1988) has summarised the findings from a large number of surveys and points out that approximately 30% of patients report dissatisfaction with the quality and amount of information they are given. This figure holds true for both hospitals and the community. Further, there is no indication of any improvement in the problem over the years. Ley (1989) suggests that some of the dissatisfaction expressed rests on the fact that patients and clients do not remember information they are given. A number of studies have shown that a considerable amount of advice and information is forgotten even when given to obtain informed consent to particular medical procedures. Cassileth *et al.* (1980) found, for example, that 200 cancer patients recalled on average 69% of the information that was offered to obtain their consent for treatment.

Although some of the forgetting may be due to anxiety and lack of familiarity with health care terminology, it is worth noting that a similar degree of information loss can be found in analogue studies undertaken with healthy volunteers (e.g. Ley, 1972). Research into human memory suggests some reasons why this might be the case. Postman and Phillips (1965) demonstrated that when there is a delay between hearing a list of words and recalling those words, recall of the early words is superior to recall of the later ones. This is known as a primacy effect. Ley and Spelman (1967) have reported a similar finding with recall of medical information. Some small-scale replications of Ley and Spelman's findings have been reported (e.g. Wattley and Müller, 1984), but using single words rather than statements. It seems worthwhile, therefore, to attempt to replicate the results using full statements giving health care information. It is expected that participants will be able to recall more initial statements giving health care information than later statements.

METHOD

Design
The independent variable was the position of items in the list and the dependent variable the number of items correctly recalled for each list position. Each participant was given a total score for the number of items correctly recalled from the first six and the last six list positions. The design can be regarded as repeated-measures with two treatment conditions. The same list of items was used for all participants, but the list was divided into two halves and the set of items appearing first was counterbalanced across participants.

Participants
Eighteen people took part in the experiment (mean age 33 years; age range 25–42 years). Fourteen of the participants were female and four male. None had a background in either nursing or medicine. An opportunity or convenience sample was used.

Materials
A list of 12 health-care-related statements was used. These were as follows:

1 You have a venous ulcer.
2 A zinc dressing has been used in the past.
3 A pinch skin graft might be helpful.
4 Do not worry if you cannot move around a great deal.
5 You should wear elastic stockings once the ulcer has healed.
6 The ulcer must be cleaned with a saline solution.

7   A district nurse is responsible for your care.
8   A four-layer bandage will be used in future.
9   Your foot may swell slightly because of the compression.
10   Your leg must be re-bandaged each week.
11   The compression exerted by the bandage will be measured at
     intervals.
12   Adhesive plaster will not be necessary.

For the alternative list, items 7 to 12 became items 1 to 6, and items 1
to 6 became 7 to 12.

Procedure

Participants were tested individually in a quiet room. They were assigned
randomly to one of the two list orders. The following instructions were
read out.

'I will read you a list of statements which might be made to a patient with
a fairly common medical condition. There will then be a delay of ten
minutes. Once the ten minutes are up, you will be asked to write down
as many of the statements as you can recall in any order that you like. Do
you have any questions?'

The twelve statements were then read out at a steady pace, the entire
sequence taking approximately 45 seconds. There was a ten-minute
delay period before recall during which the participant was encouraged
to talk in order to prevent rehearsal of the list items. Written recall was
then requested as follows:

'Please will you now write down as many of the statements as you can
recall in any order that you like. You may not be able to recall the exact
wording, but you should try to get as close to it as you can. You have five
minutes.'

At the end of the five minutes the paper was removed and the purpose
of the experiment explained fully.

RESULTS

As shown in *Table 1*, there was a clear tendency for the first items in the
list to be recalled more accurately than later items. The raw data are
included in Appendix 1.

List position	Mean items recalled	Range
1–6	2.8	2
7–12	0.8	3

Table 1: Mean number of items recalled and ranges from early and late list positions

The percentage of items correctly recalled was plotted against pairs of list
position as shown in *Figure 1*. Correct recall decreased from
approximately 70% for list positions 1 and 2 to 28% for positions 5 and
6, demonstrating a clear primacy effect.

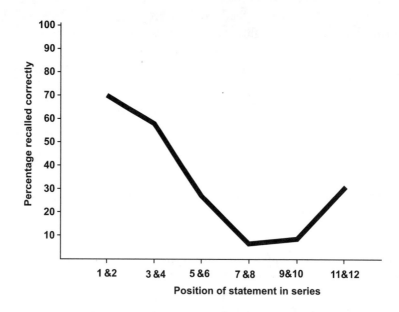

Figure 1: Percentage of items correctly recalled for pairs of list positions

The data were analysed further by comparing the total scores of individuals for the first six and the last six items. A sign test was employed and the difference was found to be highly significant at the 0.0005 level (S=0; N=17; sign test; one-tailed hypothesis). The calculations for the test are included in Appendix 2.

DISCUSSION

In this study nearly all the participants recalled more items from the beginning of the list than from the end. On average, approximately three out of the first six items were recalled accurately, but only one out of the last six. The superior recall of early items can be seen clearly in *Figure 1* and a highly significant difference was found in recall scores between early and late list positions.

These findings provide clear support for the experimental hypothesis and suggest that the order of presentation of statements intended to convey health care information has a marked effect on memory for those statements. The primacy effect that was obtained is very similar to that demonstrated by Ley and Spelman (1967) and Wattley and Müller (1984). Clearly, recall of medical information is far from perfect in healthy volunteers. This suggests that the forgetting which has often been recorded in patients in clinical situations may be due to problems of human memory as well as to anxiety and stress.

Although full statements rather than single medical terms were deliberately chosen for use in this experiment, the choice did present some drawbacks. Because the statements were intended to represent those that might be made to a patient by a practitioner, the order of the statements had to be logical. Ideally, the order of presentation should have been randomised. This would have served to guard against the possibility that more memorable items appeared at the start of the list and more difficult items at the end. Because only two orders of presentation were used, the memorability of items may have been partly or wholly responsible for the findings obtained. The study should, therefore, be replicated using different materials.

Even so, the considerable accord between this study and other studies suggests that the findings are due, at least in part, to the order in which the items were presented. The use of healthy volunteers and a fairly restricted age range may, however, restrict the extent to which the findings can be generalised. Older people may, for example, have different or additional difficulties with both the storage and the retrieval of medical information.

Furthermore, in analogue studies such as this, volunteers are asked to recall information which is not personally relevant for them. Nonetheless, as Ley (1988) points out there is a remarkable similarity between the success with which real patients remember what they are told and the recall of volunteers in analogue studies, both in the amount recalled and in the presence of primacy effects.

Overall, this study seems to confirm the idea that a considerable amount of information offered to patients will not be retained. Moreover, if early information is recalled best, then there is no guarantee that the most important items will be the ones that are remembered. Even though the forgetting may reflect a basic feature of human memory, it is likely that the problem is made worse by lack of familiarity with medical terminology. Ley (1989) suggests that memory, understanding, satisfaction and compliance are all strongly interrelated. It seems important, therefore, for health care practitioners to be aware of the potential problems and to try to ensure that information given is both understood and remembered.

REFERENCES

Cassileth, B., Zupkis, R., Sutton-Smith, K. and March, V. (1980) 'Informed consent – why are its goals improperly realised?'. *New England Journal of Medicine*, 302, pp. 896–900.

Ley, P. (1972) 'Primacy, rated importance and the recall of medical information', *Journal of Health and Social Behaviour*, 13, pp. 311–317.

Ley, P. (1988) *Communicating with Patients: Improving communication, satisfaction and compliance*, Croom Helm.

Ley, P. (1989) 'Improving patients' understanding, recall, satisfaction and compliance', in Broome, A. (ed.) *Health Psychology*, Chapman and Hall.

Ley, P. and Spelman, M. (1967) *Communicating with the Patient*, Staples Press.

Postman, L. and Phillips, L. (1965) 'Short-term temporal changes in free recall', *Quarterly Journal of Experimental Psychology*, 17, pp. 132–138.

Wattley, L. and Müller, D. (1984) *Investigating Psychology: A practical approach for nursing*, Philadelphia: Lippincott.

APPENDIX 1: RAW DATA

List position:	1	2	3	4	5	6	7	8	9	10	11	12
People												
1	1	0	1	0	0	1	0	0	0	0	0	0
2	1	1	1	0	0	0	0	0	0	0	1	0
3	1	1	0	0	0	0	0	0	0	1	0	0
4	1	0	1	1	0	0	0	0	0	0	0	1
5	1	1	0	0	1	1	0	0	0	0	1	0
6	1	1	0	1	0	0	0	0	0	0	0	0
7	0	0	1	1	1	0	0	0	0	0	0	1
8	1	1	1	0	0	0	0	0	0	0	0	0
9	1	0	1	0	0	1	0	0	0	0	0	0
10	1	1	0	1	0	1	0	0	0	0	0	0
11	0	0	1	1	1	0	0	0	0	0	0	1
12	1	0	1	1	0	0	0	0	0	0	1	0
13	1	0	1	0	0	1	0	1	0	0	0	1
14	1	1	0	1	0	0	0	0	0	1	0	1
15	1	1	1	0	0	0	0	0	0	0	1	0
16	1	0	1	1	0	0	0	0	0	0	1	0
17	1	1	0	1	0	0	0	0	0	0	0	0
18	0	1	1	0	0	1	0	1	0	1	0	1

APPENDIX 2: STATISTICAL CALCULATIONS

Sign test

List position/	1–6	7–12	Difference
People			
1	3	0	+3
2	3	1	+2
3	2	1	+1
4	3	1	+2
5	4	1	+3
6	3	0	+3
7	3	1	+2
8	3	0	+3
9	3	0	+3
10	4	0	+4
11	3	1	+2
12	3	1	+2
13	3	2	+1
14	3	2	+1
15	3	1	+2
16	3	1	+2
17	3	0	+3
18	3	3	0
			+ = 17
			− = 0

$$S = 0; N = 17; p < 0.0005, \text{one-tailed}$$

Writing an abstract

Now have a try at writing an abstract for our study.

ACTIVITY 22   ALLOW 20 MINUTES

Read carefully through the practical report given above. Then write an abstract for it in no more than 200 words. Be sure to include a statement about:

- what was done
- what was found
- what conclusions, if any, were drawn.

Commentary

You might like to compare your version with the one that I came up with.

ABSTRACT

Eighteen healthy volunteers were presented with a list of 12 statements conveying health care information. Written free recall was requested after a delay of ten minutes. Items which appeared in the first six list positions were recalled significantly better than items from the last six positions. The implications of the results for professional practice are considered.

The style of an experimental report

You may well have noticed in reading the entire report that the style in which it is written is rather formal. Because the intention of a report is to communicate the details of a study clearly and unambiguously, a terse, precise and impersonal style is usually adopted. Clegg (1982) offers a list of five guidelines on writing style for research reports and these are summarised below.

1   Write in complete sentences and not in note form.

2   Avoid using the first person ('I' and 'we') and try to remain neutral and objective in tone.

3   Avoid the use of slang or colloquial expressions.

4   Avoid referring to people of unspecified sex as 'he'. For example, replace 'A participant may believe that his performance . . . ' with 'Participants may believe that their performance . . . '.

5   You may use abbreviations such as IV and DV for independent and dependent variable respectively, but the first time the term is used in the report it should be given in full with the abbreviation in brackets immediately afterwards.

I realise that the wealth of details relating to report writing we have covered may make the task seem rather formidable. Although your initial attempts may require some effort, you will find that your use of the conventions rapidly becomes fairly automatic with practice. In the section below there is a checklist that you can use to guide the writing of any experimental practical report you produce in the future.

3: Preparing reports - checks and reminders

Although we have already identified and discussed the functions of each section of a research report, you might find it helpful to have a list of questions that you can check through whenever you write an experimental report. Note that the results section deals only with numerical data since this is the kind of data on which we have focused.

TITLE
Does your title indicate precisely the nature of the topic being investigated?

Have you drawn attention to any important features of the study?

ABSTRACT
Does your abstract cover the participants, independent and dependent variable(s) and design?

Have you described the main findings of the experiment and any conclusions drawn?

Have you given a clear impression of the research in less than 200 words?

INTRODUCTION
Have you conveyed the nature, source and importance of the research question?

Have you examined relevant research and explained why previous studies do not provide a complete answer to the question?

Have you made your experimental hypothesis clear?

METHOD

Design
Have you noted if the experiment is a field study or a partial experiment of some kind?

Have you identified the independent and dependent variables, the treatment conditions and whether the design uses repeated measures or independent samples?

Have you noted any attempts to identify and control extraneous variables?

Participants
Does your account make it clear how they were obtained?

Have you given the numbers and all relevant details?

Materials

Have you described any materials used clearly?

Have you included the actual materials where appropriate?

Have you put any lengthy word lists or similar details into an appendix?

Procedure

Does your account state exactly what the researcher did and exactly what the participants experienced?

Have you included, either here or in an appendix, the precise instructions that were given?

Is there sufficient detail for your procedure to be replicated precisely by another researcher?

RESULTS

Have you provided a summary or summaries of the data showing totals, averages and dispersion of scores for each treatment condition?

Are the raw data included in an appendix?

Have you made full use of figures to provide visual impact?

Are all the tables and figures clearly labelled?

Have you made it clear what statistical test(s) was used, why it was used and with what result (significance level; one- or two-tailed)?

Have you included the statistical calculations in an appendix?

DISCUSSION

Have you described the important features of the results and analyses clearly?

Have you noted the extent to which your results support your experimental hypothesis and how they relate to the aims of the study?

Are possible explanations for the results fully explored?

Have you drawn clear conclusions from your findings and indicated directions for future research?

Have you considered the implications of your findings for professional practice?

REFERENCES

Are all studies, books and articles cited in the text included in alphabetical order?

I hope that you find this checklist useful. You might like to try it out on the specimen report given in section 2.

Do bear in mind how important it is for the results of research to be clearly communicated. Sound and interesting research may have little impact on professional practice and the care of patients or clients if readers have to struggle to discover what was done, what was found and what conclusions may be drawn. As Hockey (1991) points out:

'Many members of the nursing profession fail to see, or do not wish to see, the importance of research and only perseverance and demonstration of its worth can be expected to change their attitude. Sometimes their lack of interest or enthusiasm is at least partially the fault of researchers who fail to communicate appropriately with their peer groups. The communication of research is as important as the research itself.'

Summary

1   The title of an experimental report should convey the nature of the investigation and any noteworthy features of the study.

2   An abstract should provide sufficient information for readers to decide whether they wish to continue with the rest of the report.

3   The distinctive style of a research report is intended to ensure precision, clarity and objectivity in reporting and discussing the study.

4   If research findings are not communicated clearly, their potential impact on professional practice may be lost.

Before you move on to Session Seven, check that you have achieved the objectives given at the beginning of this session, and, if not, review the appropriate sections.

Experiment II: planning the study

Introduction

In this session and those that follow, we will be planning, carrying out, analysing and interpreting a second small-scale experiment. As before, you will be guided through the process, and data that I have gathered will be supplied in case you are unable to carry out all of the study yourself. I will, however, ask you to write the majority of the report and get feedback on it from your tutor. In order to consolidate and extend your knowledge and understanding, the design and statistical analysis will be slightly different from the study that we have just completed. By the time you have completed your report, you should have a good grasp of the basic principles of conducting and reporting small-scale experimental research.

Session objectives

When you have completed this session, you should be able to:

- decide on the procedure for conducting an experiment

- draft the introductory section to an experimental report.

1: Asking the research question

An additional source of research questions

Our first task is to identify a suitable research question. You may remember that in Session Two we listed five possible sources of research questions. They were as follows:

- your own experience

- professional literature

- theoretical frameworks

- conferences and study days

- national directives and Delphi studies.

Can you now add another possibility to this list? Experiments you carry out yourself can generate ideas for further research. This can happen in at least three ways. First, the process of planning the experiment encourages you to look carefully and critically at the previous literature. Second, conducting the research allows you to observe and talk to the people who are taking part. Third, in order to interpret the results you have to analyse the strengths and weaknesses of the design and procedure that you have used.

It is worth remembering that one of the advantages of the experimental approach, in contrast to large-scale surveys, for example, is that it usually brings you into direct contact with participants both as they are taking part in the research and after the study has been completed. Did you get any ideas about our experiment from observing and talking to the two people that you recruited? You may, for example, have spotted some potential problems with the procedure or materials, or have discovered that some individuals adopt specific strategies to try to remember the statements in the list. Observations such as these, although they do not provide conclusive evidence, can be extremely useful and can be mentioned in the discussion section of the report.

In order to gain some practice, look back over the study that we have completed and see if you can identify some further questions for experimental research that it generates. Because of ethical considerations, I suggest that you restrict your ideas to studies that could be carried out with healthy volunteers. Analogue studies, such as the one that we conducted, can be very useful for a number of purposes, and it is often well worth considering if research with real patients or clients can be avoided, at least in the preliminary stages of a research project.

ACTIVITY 23   ALLOW **10** MINUTES

Think about or look back to the study we have just completed. Did any ideas for further research occur to you while we were designing, planning, analysing or interpreting the study? Did you get any ideas from observing or talking to your participants? Note down these ideas. Can you think of any other possible research questions which stem either from our study or from the background literature that we discussed? Note these ideas down as well.

Commentary

How did you get on? Given below are some possibilities that occurred to me:

- would fewer statements produce a different pattern of recall and/or better recall?
- would a reduction in the amount of medical terminology produce a different pattern of recall and/or better recall?
- is there any effect of age on the amount recalled or the pattern of recall?
- what would be the effect of a longer delay period before recall?
- would different sets of health care statements give the same pattern of results?
- would repetition of the list of statements help recall?

The study that we conducted and the activity above should have served to emphasise the importance of replicating previous research. Replication not only helps to confirm the accuracy and generality of research findings, it may also give you important insights into possible alternative interpretations of the results. Even though our study was not a complete replication of Ley and Spelman (1967), it should have helped you to think about why both healthy volunteers and patients or clients in clinical settings tend to experience difficulties recalling particular portions of the information that they are offered.

Identifying the research question

We still, however, need to identify a research question for the next study. In reading the literature on patient forgetting, I came across an intriguing comment by Ley (1989). He notes that:

'One final peculiarity of the results of studies of patients' forgetting is worth mentioning. This is that there seems to be no tendency for forgetting to increase with the passage of time. What patients can recall shortly after the consultation they tend to retain for a considerable time'.

(Ley, 1989)

The 'peculiarity' of these results is that they seem to conflict with many of the findings on human memory. Baddley points out that typically:

'information loss is very rapid at first and then levels off . . . [this] holds good for many types of learned material.'

(Baddley, 1982)

There appears, therefore, to be a discrepancy between the forgetting of health-care-related information and the forgetting of other kinds of material. There are a number of reasons why this discrepancy might occur. For example, perhaps there is less forgetting of personally relevant information. See if you can think of any other possible explanations.

ACTIVITY 24   ALLOW **10 MINUTES**

Ley (1989) identified an apparent 'peculiarity' in the findings of studies of patients' forgetting. Note down any possible explanations that you can think of for why this 'peculiarity' might occur. Note also if you could check any of those explanations by examining the details of the studies that Ley commented on.

Commentary

When I came across Ley's (1989) statement, three possible explanations occurred to me. These are given below along with the details that I would want to check in the original studies.

1   Perhaps forgetting is different for personally relevant information? Check if the studies were carried out with patients or with healthy volunteers.

2   Perhaps the patients were asked to recall after the consultation as well as after a long delay and this procedure consolidated their memory for the information? Check the designs used – were they repeated measures or independent samples in which different groups of individuals recalled after different delay periods?

3   Perhaps the patients were given information about the course of their illness, treatment or side-effects of treatment which they might later recall from experience rather than from the information given? Check if there are any analogue studies producing similar results.

Ley (1988) describes the studies that he was commenting on in some detail. The great majority of the studies were carried out with patients in clinical settings, but only one appears to have used repeated measures with the same patients (Muss *et al.* 1980). This being the case, it is possible that the 'peculiarity' of the findings rests either on the personal relevance of the information given, or on later experiences of the condition or the treatment.

One analogue investigation is, however, described (Ley, 1972) and in this study one group of participants was tested immediately and another after a twenty-minute delay. Those people tested immediately recalled 58 per cent of the information, and those tested after the delay period 56 per cent. This finding is remarkable since recall of verbal material tends to decline very rapidly over the first twenty minutes after the original presentation (Baddley, 1982).

If this finding can be replicated it is of considerable importance and interest. It suggests that although a considerable amount of health care information is forgotten (Ley, 1988), that which is retained is unusually resistant to forgetting. The reason or reasons why this 'peculiarity' might occur is intriguing, but the first step is to attempt to repeat Ley's (1972) original finding. Can you now identify a possible research question?

ACTIVITY 25   ALLOW 5 MINUTES

Using the background material that has been discussed above, note down the research question we could address.

Commentary

Although a number of different research questions could potentially arise from the background material that has been examined, it is essential to try to replicate Ley's finding. The research question that we will be looking at, therefore, is 'Does the length of the delay before recall affect the forgetting of health-care-related information?'. In the next section we will translate this research question into the design of an experiment.

2: From the research question to the experimental design

Specifying and varying the independent variable

This part of the process will probably feel reasonably familiar to you by now. It is, I think, still worth checking the design against the decision chart from the final session of Unit One. You may well find that you want to modify or amend the chart in various ways to remind yourself of particular issues, but a version of it will help to ensure that you consider all the essential design features.

As we have done before, we will start by specifying the independent variable and deciding how it will be varied within our study.

ACTIVITY 26   ALLOW **10** MINUTES

Look back to the research question and identify the predicted cause it contains. Specify the independent variable and consider how it might be varied in the experiment. Remember that we do not have to restrict ourselves to only two treatment conditions. If you find it helpful, you might like to start to draw up a diagrammatic representation of the design in the form that we have used previously. That is:

	Stage 1	Stage 2	and so on
Condition 1			
Condition 2			
and so on.			

Commentary

From the research question we identified, the independent variable is 'length of delay before recall'. This independent variable must be varied in terms of 'amount' and it seems sensible to retain the two levels that Ley (1972) used, that is, immediate and twenty-minutes delay, in order to form a basis for comparison of the original and the replication. We could add to this a variety of different delay periods: using periods of a week or more would certainly add to the ecological validity of the findings. Did you think about this issue?

We are, however, restricted by two considerations. First, and this is true for any study which extends over a period of time, some of the participants may be unable to return for testing. If this happens, then there is a danger that the remaining sample is biased in some way. Perhaps, for example, only people who are not very busy (and may therefore forget less) would be able to return for testing. Second, as you may have realised from the discussion of the background literature, we will inevitably be using independent samples rather than repeated measures. If we set up a large number of treatment conditions, then we will have to find large numbers of people to take part.

For these two reasons, I suggest that we add only one more delay condition. Although recall of verbal material declines very rapidly over the first twenty minutes after the original presentation, there is nonetheless a marked decline over the first hour (Baddley, 1982). Thereafter, the rate of loss tends to level off. It therefore seems reasonable to include a treatment condition in which recall is requested one hour after the original presentation. So, diagrammatically, we have:

	Stage 1	Stage 2	and so on

Condition 1 – Immediate
Condition 2 – 20-minute delay
Condition 3 – 60-minute delay

Treatment conditions and people

As we have already noted, different people will be asked to experience the three different conditions. This experiment is a very good example of one of the principles that we identified in Unit One for deciding between a repeated-measures and an independent-samples design. Can you remember what it was? We noted that you cannot use a repeated-measures design when the experience of a particular treatment condition may produce a change in the person who experiences it. In this experiment, if an individual recalled the material immediately and was then tested again after twenty or sixty minutes, the later scores might well be affected by the earlier attempt.

The danger, as you may remember, of using independent samples is that the groups may differ in terms of some relevant variable such as memory ability. How do you deal with this possibility? Although one option might be to match the individuals in the three groups for memory, we cannot be sure that this is the only relevant variable. The usual strategy is to offer the treatment conditions to individuals on an entirely random basis and this is the option that we will adopt. So, our design now looks like this:

	Stage 1	Stage 2

Condition 1 – Immediate
Group 1

Condition 2 – 20-minute delay
Group 2

Condition 3 – 60-minute delay
Group 3

Control of extraneous variables

Can you think of any extraneous variables that need to be controlled? As in our previous experiment, we will need to ensure that as many aspects of the situation as possible are held constant for the three different groups. The kind of features we identified previously were:

- instructions given to the participants
- time of day
- level of noise
- material to be remembered
- rate of presentation of material.

In this case, we will try to hold all the variables constant apart from time of day. Since we will only be looking at the total number of items recalled, the same materials can be used with all participants.

In this design, we also need to be particularly careful to ensure that the presentation and recall conditions are the same for all three groups. The experiment would be confounded if, for example, you tested all of the people in the one-hour delay condition first when you were relatively unpractised at carrying out the study. You must also take great care not to let people know the level of recall that you expect them to produce. Think back to Session Four of Unit One where it was noted that a researcher can introduce constant error into the results of an experiment by inadvertently treating one group of individuals differently from another.

Measurement of the effect

The dependent variable that we will use is, as has been mentioned, the number of items recalled. As for the first experiment, the scale of measurement is interval. Overall, our design is as follows:

	Stage 1	Stage 2	Stage 3
Condition 1 – Immediate Group 1	Material presented to all participants individually	No delay	Free recall of material
Condition 2 – 20-minute delay Group 2	Material presented to all participants individually	20-minute delay	Free recall of material
Condition 3 – 60-minute delay Group 3	Material presented to all participants individually	60-minute delay	Free recall of material

Stating the experimental hypothesis

Now have a try at writing an experimental hypothesis for the study. You will need to bear in mind that the vast majority of work would lead us to predict that recall will differ with different delay intervals.

ACTIVITY 27   ALLOW 5 MINUTES

Write down an experimental hypothesis for the study we have designed. Bear in mind that, although we can assume that recall will differ with different delay, we cannot confidently predict that the twenty-minute delay will be worse than the immediate, and that the sixty-minute delay will be worse than the twenty-minute.

Is it a one-tailed or two-tailed hypothesis?

Commentary

My version of the experimental hypothesis is:

'There will be a significant difference in the recall of health-care-related information between immediate recall and delays of 20 and 60 minutes between presentation and recall.'

When you write a hypothesis for an experiment with three or more treatment conditions, you have only two choices. You can predict either that:

● there will be a difference between the conditions

or

● there will be a consistent trend in one direction.

The former hypothesis is two-tailed and the latter one-tailed. In this case, we cannot confidently predict a consistent trend and so we cannot use a one-tailed hypothesis. All we can do, therefore, is to predict that recall will be different with different delay periods, so our hypothesis is two-tailed.

Choosing a statistical test

In the first experiment, a sign test was used to analyse the data. This test can be used when two treatment conditions are compared and the scores in each are related. It is not suitable for this experiment, since we have three treatment conditions and unrelated scores. The appropriate statistical test to analyse our data is known as the Kruskal-Wallis test. Since we have no reason to be particularly cautious in setting the significance level, we will adopt the usual level of 0.05.

3: Working out the procedure

When we designed our first study, we did not consider the procedural details until after the introduction to the report had been presented. The reason behind this was to illustrate how different kinds of detail are slotted into the different sections of a report. However, as you will probably have realised, I had considered all of the details of the experiment before writing the introduction. This time we will flesh out the basic structure of the study before moving on to write the introduction.

I suggest that you have a try at filling out the details yourself and then compare your decisions with the ones I have made. Remember that we already have a list of statements intended to convey health care information which could be adapted in some way. Also bear in mind that you will be selecting a sample of people to take part yourself.

ACTIVITY 28   ALLOW **20** MINUTES

Look back to section 1 in Session Three in which we finalised the details of our first study. Carry out the same process for the present experiment and note down the decisions that you make. Remember that you need to consider:

- participants – sampling? number? other requirements?
- materials – number of items to be used?
- procedure – random allocation? informed consent?

Commentary

Given below are the ideas that I came up with and the decisions that I made when I ran the study myself.

1 Participants

I collected data from 18 people – six in each group. The age range was 21 to 38 years, 12 were female and all the participants were student volunteers. None of them were taking health care courses and none had a nursing or medical background. I am aware that the sample is small but suggest that you restrict yours to much the same size. You will, though, have to consider the problems that this causes when you come to interpret your results.

2 Materials

I used a similar list of items to those in the first study. The advantage is that we now know what level of recall is likely to be achieved with these materials. With a delay of ten minutes we found that people recalled about three to four items. Since we are going to introduce even longer delay periods, there is the danger of a floor effect in this case – none of the material might be recalled at all. Consequently, I reduced the number of items to ten and also simplified them slightly. The list I came up with is as follows:

1 You have an ulcer on your leg.
2 A zinc dressing has been used on it.
3 A different bandage will be used in future.
4 The ulcer must be cleaned with saline.
5 A district nurse will come to see you.
6 Your leg must be looked at each week.
7 Your foot may swell slightly.
8 You may not be able to move around easily.
9 The ulcer should heal completely.
10 Elastic stockings will be helpful.

If you have time, you might like **to pilot** or test your materials with about ten people to check that they do produce a level of recall which is reasonable for your purposes.

You will also need writing materials for your participants as before.

To pilot: materials or procedures that are piloted are tested on a relatively small sample of people to ensure that they will work efficiently in the study

3 Procedure

In order to obtain a small sample of people who are willing to take part, you should explain that you are carrying out a simple study of memory for health care information and that names will not be recorded. You should ensure that they are available to recall the information at any time during the hour after presentation if necessary. In this way, consent will have been given to all of the conditions and you do not need to make your participants aware that they have been assigned to one particular condition.

You can then randomly allocate the people to the treatment conditions. The easiest way to achieve this is to write 'Immediate', '20' or '60' on bits of paper (six of each if you use 18 people) and draw one out of a bag for each person.

As before, you will need a quiet room in which to conduct the study and each person must be seen individually. The precise instructions which I gave to participants are noted below.

'I will read you a list of statements which might be made to a patient with a fairly common medical condition. When I have read the list, you will be asked to write down as many of the statements as you can recall in any order that you like. Do you have any questions?'

Remember to read the statements at a steady pace. You should practise first and find out how long the list takes to read. For the delay conditions, I suggest that you let people get on with whatever they were doing and ask them to come back about five minutes before the delay period is up. You can then ask for recall of the items by saying,

'Please will you now write down as many of the statements as you can recall in any order that you like. You may not be able to recall the exact wording, but you should try to get as close to it as you can. You have five minutes.'

When each person has finished you should be prepared to discuss any aspects of the study that the participant wants to talk about. Do remember to ensure that nobody leaves feeling that they have done badly in any way.

Having compared your ideas with mine, you may want to adopt a procedure which is slightly different from the one that I used. Feel free to do so provided you can justify your decisions and provided you do not alter the basic design. If your study is radically different from mine, then the guidelines that I give for data analysis will not apply.

4: Writing your report - the introduction

I realise that you may want to get on with running the study at this point, but I suggest very strongly that you stop now and write a rough draft of your introduction. This will help you to check that the line of argument leading to the study is clear and logical. It should also prevent important details being forgotten. Clegg (1982) makes a similar point rather nicely. She urges:

'Always make the attempt to write up your report as soon as possible after you have conducted the work – and certainly within days, rather than weeks. Otherwise you will confirm for yourself the amazing rapidity with which unrehearsed and unorganised material is forgotten.'

Do you remember the way in which the introduction to a report was likened to a funnel? Essentially, this means that you should cover:

- the general subject area
- relevant theory and research work
- the particular predictions to be tested
- the specific hypothesis.

I will give you a start by covering the general subject area, and then ask you to complete the rest of the introduction yourself. Although you may want to make use of articles and books that I have not mentioned, all of the material that you need to write the introduction is contained in this session. I suggest that you take brief notes of any points you want to include and a copy of any quotations you want to use, and then put the unit away while you write. This will help you to check your understanding of the material and to put the ideas into your own words. You might begin the introduction in the following way:

INTRODUCTION

Lack of information is a source of anxiety for large numbers of patients and clients in both hospital and community settings. Not only is this level of dissatisfaction a cause of concern in its own right, but there is also a body of evidence linking the lack of satisfaction to lack of compliance with health care advice (Ley, 1988).

Ley (1988) points out that although the appropriate information may be provided by health care practitioners, some of it may not be understood and much of it is certainly forgotten. Studies of real patients in clinical settings and analogue studies with healthy volunteers both report that only about half of the health care information that is given is accurately recalled.

In reality, however, it may be over-optimistic to expect as much as half of the information given to be retained. Many patients and clients have to remember health care advice over long periods of time, and even more forgetting may occur.

ACTIVITY 29

Complete a *first draft* of the introduction section for our experiment. In Session Eleven you will be asked to pull the complete report together, and this will give you the opportunity to polish off any rough edges. You can use the three paragraphs given in the box above as the starting point, but don't feel obliged to do so.

Commentary

How did you get on? If you are working with other students you might like to swap drafts at this point and give each other some feedback on the progress so far.

You may be wondering how long an introduction ought to be. This is a very difficult question to answer since it depends entirely on what it is you have to say. The only sensible guidance I can give is to suggest that you check that each and every point you have included is clearly relevant to the study you are going to carry out. If you are reasonably happy that this is the case, then the length can be left to look after itself.

Summary

1 The process of designing, conducting and interpreting a piece of experimental research may generate questions for further research.

2 The Kruskal-Wallis test is an appropriate statistical test when there are three treatment conditions and unrelated scores.

3 The three crucial aspects to consider in working out the details of an experiment are participants, materials and procedure.

4 The introduction to a study should be drafted once decisions relating to design and procedure have been made, even if it is revised after the data are collected. This practice can serve as a check that the rationale for the study is clear and logical and it ensures that details are not forgotten.

Before you move on to Session Eight, check that you have achieved the objectives given at the beginning of this session, and, if not, review the appropriate sections.

Experiment II: carrying out the study

Introduction

In this session you will be asked to conduct the experiment that has just been designed. I will outline the steps that you need to carry out in the form of a checklist, and then ask you to test the sample of people that you recruit. Most of your time for this session, therefore, will be spent on this activity. If, for any reason, you are unable to carry out the study yourself, you can make use of the data that I collected which will be given in the next session. You will also be asked to complete a draft of the method section while the procedural details are fresh in your mind.

Session objectives

When you have completed this session, you should be able to:

- Prepare and conduct a small-scale experiment of your own with supervision

- draft the method section of an experimental report.

1: Collecting the data

Final preparations

You may at this point feel rather daunted by the prospect of recruiting and testing a total of 18 people. There are, however, a number of strategies that you can use to reduce the amount of work involved. You could try one of the following options.

1 Work in a group with other students and combine your data. If you do this do not run one condition each – this would have the effect of turning you all into a confounding variable!

2 Conduct part of the experiment yourself and combine your data with mine. Again take care to test people in all three conditions. Also remember to match your participants and procedure as closely to mine as you can.

3 Test only four or five people in each condition. Since the sample I have suggested is already rather small for an independent-groups design, you will reduce the sensitivity of the experiment still further. This is acceptable for a practice experiment, provided that you state the limitations very clearly and explicitly in the discussion.

Assuming that you have decided how many people you intend to test, you can now continue with the basic preparation.

ACTIVITY 30   ALLOW **60** MINUTES

Use the checklist below to get ready to conduct the experiment.

1 Check that you understand the study well enough to be able to explain its rationale to the people that you test.

2 Make clear copies of the list of statements to be read out and the instructions to be used for each condition.

3 Identify a quiet room that you can use.

4 Practise reading the list of statements at a slow and steady pace.

5 Make sure that you have writing materials for the participants and a way to time the delay and recall periods.

6 Identify a sample of people who are willing to take part. Randomly assign each person to one of the three treatment conditions. Then arrange a time for each person to be tested individually. If you do things in this order then you should be able to test people in the 'Immediate' or '20-minute delay' conditions during the 60-minute delay for other participants.

Commentary

Although the total time that you spend in testing people will not be great, the delay periods will entail a fairly tight schedule. You will probably find it easiest to spread the testing across several days to ensure that you do not make mistakes or have to rush anyone through either recall or debriefing. Please do not be tempted to skimp on any of the details. Carrying out experimental research can be demanding, but the attention to detail is essential.

Conducting the experiment

You should now be ready to start the testing stage.

ACTIVITY 31   ALLOW 3 HOURS

Use the checklist below to carry out the experiment.

1 Read out the appropriate set of instructions and answer any questions.

2 Read out the list of statements.

3 Time the delay period if there should be one.

4 Ask for recall using the written set of instructions. Time the five-minute recall period.

5 Explain the purpose of the study and be prepared to discuss any aspect. Ask the participants for their reactions and record any comments.

6 *Make a note on the recall sheet about the condition that the person experienced.* If you forget to do this you will be unable to sort out which data belongs to which condition.

7 Make a note of any ideas about the experiment that occur to you.

Commentary

I hope that the study went well for you. It should have helped you to appreciate the real value of a pilot study. Pilot studies allow you to check not only any materials that you are using, but also all of the procedural details. Furthermore, even if you find that you do not need to adjust any of those details, a pilot gives you an opportunity to practise your part. You may well have found in this practical that your 'performance' became progressively smoother as you tested more people. In other words, your level of skill was an extraneous variable. A pilot study would have allowed this variable to have been held constant or nearly constant for the actual experiment because the rate of improvement would have slowed considerably.

2: Writing your research report - the method

You are now in the position to write a draft of the method section of the report. You might like to look back to section 3 in Session Three where we discussed the separate components of the method section and the detail that should be included in each. You will find that this practical is quite close to the one that we carried out previously.

The section which often causes the most problems is 'Design'. You might like to make use of the skeleton that I have provided below.

METHOD

Design

In this experiment the independent variable was . . . and the dependent variable was . . . . Three levels of the independent variable were used which were . . . . An independent-samples design was employed and participants were randomly allocated to one of the three treatment conditions. The same list of items . . . .

Now have a go at writing a first draft of the entire method section.

ACTIVITY 32 ALLOW **30** MINUTES

Complete a first draft of the method section for our experiment. Remember the four subsections are:

- design
- participants
- materials
- procedure.

Try to keep your style concise and include only the essential details with no discussion. You will probably find that you have rather too many sets of instructions to be included comfortably in this section. I suggest that you put them in an appendix – but do remember to tell your readers where to find them.

Commentary

By this point you have completed a really substantial part of the practical and gained some very useful experience. You will probably appreciate how essential it is to have help and guidance in planning and conducting research. Even very experienced researchers often work in teams for this reason.

In the next session you will be guided through the analysis of the data and the results section of the report.

Summary

1 Experiments can be confounded by different researchers running different treatment conditions.

2 The aim of pilot studies is to check that the design, materials and procedure fulfil the aims of the experiment. They are also a useful way for the researcher to become skilled in conducting the experiment.

3   The method section of an experimental report should not be allowed to become vague or too long. Details of materials and instructions given to participants may be included in an appendix.

Before you move on to Session Nine, check that you have achieved the objectives given at the beginning of this session, and, if not, review the appropriate section.

Experiment II: analysing the results

Introduction

The aim of this session is to guide you through the process of organising, summarising, analysing and presenting the data that you have collected. Since the design of this experiment differs in a number of ways from our first study, you will be introduced to another statistical test. This will help to consolidate your understanding of some of the basic principles of inferential statistics. You will need a calculator for this session.

Session objectives

When you have completed this session, you should be able to:

- organise, summarise and analyse the data from an experiment

- draft the results section of a report.

1: Organising the data

The stages for description and analysis

Just to remind you, there are four essential stages that you must go through before you can present the findings from an experiment. You have to:

1   Obtain a score or scores for each person taking part in the study. This may involve adding or averaging two or more actual scores obtained by that individual.
2   Organise or collate the raw data in such a way that you can readily calculate measures of central tendency and dispersion and prepare tables and figures.
3   Summarise the data to illustrate clearly the effects of changes in the independent variable.
4   Use a statistical test or tests to examine the experimental hypothesis.

We will carry out the first two of these steps in this section.

Obtaining the raw data

Your first task, therefore, is to derive a score for each person who took part in the experiment. The activity below will help you with this process.

ACTIVITY 33   ALLOW **20** MINUTES

You should have a piece of paper for each participant showing the items that were recalled. Using the list that was actually read out, score each item recalled as correct or incorrect. The recall does not need to be perfect but should express the essential idea contained in the original statement. For example, for the item 'The ulcer must be cleaned with saline' you should score as correct any of the following attempts or any version which is reasonably close to them:

- the ulcer should be cleaned with saline
- the ulcer must be treated with saltwater
- the leg will be cleaned with saline
- saline will be put on the leg.

By contrast, attempts such as:

- the leg will be washed
- salt will be put on the ulcer

should be scored as incorrect.

Commentary

I found in my scoring that most of the attempts were correct. If an item had been recalled at all, then it was usually reasonably accurate. People seemed to find this set of items slightly easier than the ones we used for our first study. What did you find? Now let us move onto the next step.

Organising the raw data

ACTIVITY 34　　　　　　　　　　ALLOW **10** MINUTES

You should now total the items correctly recalled for each individual. Enter each score on a data sheet such as the one given below. Different individuals are identified as P1, P2 and so on. Since each individual was presented with ten statements, the maximum score for any one person is 10.

Group 1 Immediate	Group 2 20-minute delay	Group 3 60-minute delay
P1	P7	P13
P2	P8	P14
P3	P9	P15
P4	P10	P16
P5	P11	P17
P6	P12	P18

Provided that the scores from individuals are entered into the correct treatment condition, the order in which they are entered does not matter. The reason that I have given a number for each participant is simply to allow you to refer to an individual's score if you wish.

Commentary

The data that I obtained are given below.

Group 1 Immediate		Group 2 20-minute delay		Group 3 60-minute delay	
P1	4	**P7**	3	**P13**	3
P2	7	**P8**	4	**P14**	3
P3	5	**P9**	3	**P15**	2
P4	3	**P10**	2	**P16**	1
P5	6	**P11**	5	**P17**	4
P6	4	**P12**	3	**P18**	0

The raw data sheet that you have prepared should be included as an appendix with your practical report. In the next section we will summarise the data to bring out more clearly the pattern of results obtained.

2: Describing the data

Summarising the data

Our next step is to summarise the raw data so that they show the pattern of results we have obtained. We will, therefore, calculate a measure of central tendency and a measure of dispersion for each treatment condition. In other words, we will start by using descriptive statistics.

To Calculate a Mean
1 Add up all the scores.
2 Divide the result by the total number of scores:
e.g. 5 + 10 + 6 = 21
Mean = $\frac{21}{3}$ = 7

ACTIVITY 35   ALLOW 10 MINUTES

Calculate the mean and range for each column of scores on your raw data sheet. Enter the figures you obtain in a table such as the one given as Table 8 below.

Condition	Mean items recalled	Range
Immediate		
20-minute delay		
60-minute delay		

Table 8 Mean number of items recalled and ranges from each condition

Commentary

You should now begin to get a picture of the overall pattern of results. If your data are anything like mine, then you will find that the difference between the means looks rather small. The table that you have produced can be labelled and included in the results section of your report.

Presenting the data

We also need to consider whether the results should be presented as a figure as well. As we noted before, it usually helps the reader if you can provide a graphical representation of some kind. You can use a line graph, as we did for our previous study, but you should note that the delay intervals must be shown accurately on the horizontal axis. It should, therefore, look something like this:

```
0        20                    60
```
Delay period in minutes

What about the vertical axis? The intention is to illustrate any decrease in the number of items recalled over time. Which of the two possibilities given below do you think gives the clearest picture?

```
                  100                                        10
Percentage                              Mean
recalled           50                   recalled             5
correctly                               correctly
                   0                                         0
```

Both of these options are perfectly correct, but I think the one on the left is slightly clearer. It is very obvious to a reader that 100 per cent correctly recalled means perfect recall; it is not so immediately obvious that '10' has the same meaning. The activity below asks you to prepare a graph using the horizontal axis provided and either of the vertical axes that have been illustrated.

ACTIVITY 36

Convert the total recall scores for each condition into percentages. Then plot the percentages on a line graph. There is no need to use graph paper provided your measurements are accurate. Remember to join the three points with straight lines.

To Calculate the Percentages

1 Divide the total recall score by the maximum possible score.

2 Multiply the result by 100:

e.g. Maximum possible score for any condition with 6 participants = 60

Total correct score for 'immediate' condition = 29

$$\frac{29}{60} = 0.48$$

Percentage = 0.48 x 100
= 48%

Commentary

You now have a figure which can, when labelled, be included in your report. In the next section we will use a statistical test to decide if the findings do or do not support the experimental hypothesis.

3: Analysing the data

You will have already assembled the data in an appropriate form on your data sheet. The statistical test you will be using this time is the Kruskal-Wallis. I will list the steps that you need to take for this test with some purely imaginary figures and then ask you to repeat the process on the set of data you are using.

	Condition 1			Condition 2			Condition 3	
	Score	Rank		Score	Rank		Score	Rank
P1	27	11	P5	15	6	P9	5	2
P2	18	7	P6	20	8.5	P10	3	1
P3	7	3	P7	13	5	P11	20	8.5
P4	52	12	P8	22	10	P12	8	4

STEP 1: Give a rank to the scores from all individuals regardless of which treatment condition the score is in. The smallest score is given a rank of 1, the next 2 and so on. If any of the scores are identical, then give them the mean of the ranks they would occupy (e.g. the two scores of 20 above would use ranks 8 and 9 – so they are both given rank 8.5).

STEP 2: Add up the ranks for each condition separately to produce X, Y and Z.

X = 33 Y = 29.5 Z = 15.5

STEP 3: Using your calculator, square each total to produce X^2 and so on.

$X^2 = 1089$ $Y^2 = 870.25$ $Z^2 = 240.25$

STEP 4: Divide each of the squared totals by the number of individual scores in each condition.

$$\frac{X^2}{4} = 272.25 \qquad \frac{Y^2}{4} = 217.56 \qquad \frac{Z^2}{4} = 60.06$$

STEP 5: Then add the results obtained together.

272.5 + 217.56 + 60.06 = 549.87

STEP 6: Calculate 'H' by using the following steps. Note that N is the total number of individuals in the study.

a) Calculate N (N + 1)   e.g. 12 (13) = 12 x 13 = 156

b) Divide 12 by the above answer (always use 12 in this step regardless of the number of participants!)   e.g. $\frac{12}{156} = 0.077$

c) Multiply the above answer by the result of Step 5 above
e.g. 0.077 x 549.87 = 42.49

d) Calculate 3 (N + 1)   e.g. 3 (13) = 3 x 13 = 39

e) H = (result of Step 6.3) – (result of Step 6.4)
       e.g. 42.49 – 39 = 3.29

STEP 7: Calculate df (degrees of freedom) by subtracting 1 from the total number of treatment conditions   e.g. 3 – 1 = 2

STEP 8: Look up the significance level in the table. Two different tables for the Kruskal-Wallis have been included. *Table 9* can only be used if there are no more than five individuals in any of the treatment conditions – when this is the case you do not need to carry out Step 7.

Using *Table 9*, find the line that gives 4 in each n column (n = number of individuals in a treatment condition) and trace the line along to the relevant column, i.e. p<.05. As you can see, my value of H is not as high as those given in the table, so it is not significant at the 0.05 level. (H=3.29; n=4; Kruskal-Wallis test; two-tailed hypothesis).

(Adapted from Greene, 1990)

Group sizes (C=3)			$p<.05$ (two-tailed)	$p<.01$ (two tailed)
n_1	n_2	n_3		
3	3	3	5.6	6.5
4	3	3	5.7	6.7
4	4	3	5.6	7.1
4	4	4	5.7	7.5
5	3	3	5.5	7.0
5	4	3	5.6	7.4
5	4	4	5.6	7.7
5	5	3	5.6	7.5
5	5	4	5.6	7.8
5	5	5	5.7	8.0

Table 9 Critical values for H for various levels of significance
(no more than five individuals in any condition). The calculated value of H is
significant if it is **equal** to or **larger** than the critical value in the table.

ACTIVITY 37   ALLOW 15 MINUTES

Carry out a Kruskal-Wallis test on your data following the steps that have been described above. If you have six people in each condition, look up the significance level in *Table 10* with df = 2. (For an explanation of degrees of freedom see Clegg, 1982, pp. 88–89; Greene, 1990, p. 80.)

| | | Two-tailed test* | |
df	p<.05	p<.02	p<.01
1	3.84	5.41	6.64
2	5.99	7.82	9.21
3	7.82	9.84	11.34
4	9.49	11.67	13.28
5	11.07	13.39	15.09
6	12.59	15.03	16.81
7	14.07	16.62	18.48
8	15.51	18.17	20.09
9	16.92	19.68	21.67
10	18.31	21.16	23.21
11	19.68	22.62	24.72
12	21.03	24.05	26.22
13	22.36	25.47	27.69
14	23.68	26.87	29.14
15	25.00	28.26	30.58
16	26.30	29.63	32.00
17	27.59	31.00	33.41
18	28.87	32.35	34.80
19	30.14	33.69	36.19
20	31.41	35.02	37.57
21	32.67	36.34	38.93
22	33.92	37.66	40.29
23	35.17	38.97	41.64
24	36.42	40.27	42.98
25	37.65	41.57	44.31
26	38.88	42.86	45.64
27	40.11	44.14	46.96
28	41.34	45.42	48.28
29	42.56	46.69	49.59
30	43.77	47.96	50.86

Table 10 Critical values of H for various levels of significance
(six or more individuals in any of the conditions). The calculated value of H is
significant if it is **equal** to or **larger** than the critical value in the table.

Commentary

Is your value of H equal to or greater than the value given in the table? Your value of H would have to be equal to or greater than 5.99 in order to achieve significance at the 0.05 level. If it is not, then there is no significant difference between the treatment conditions.

You can now note down the results of your analysis as I have in brackets at the end of Step 8 and you can include the statement in your results section. Have you accepted the null hypothesis? Do your findings support the experimental hypothesis or not?

This section will have provided you with enough information to write your results section.

4: Writing your research report - the results

You now have all the material that you need to put together the results section of your report. A good way to start is by including the summary tables of totals, means and ranges that you prepared and noting briefly in the text what they seem to show. If you get stuck at any point, have a look back to the results section for the first study in section 3 of Session Four.

ACTIVITY 38   ALLOW 30 MINUTES

Complete a draft of the results section of your report. Make sure that you include:

- the descriptive statistics
- any tables or figures that you have prepared
- the results of the statistical test
- the raw data in an appendix
- the statistical calculations in an appendix.

Remember that all tables and figures must be labelled and referred to in the text even if their meaning seems obvious to you. Similarly, you should note in the text any information which has been put into appendices and where those appendices can be found.

Commentary

You have now drafted three out of the four major sections of the report. While you conducted and analysed the experiment, a number of points may have occurred to you which will be relevant for an interpretation of the results. If so, do make sure that you have a note of them since there is a danger that they will be forgotten once you get involved in the process of preparing the discussion section.

Summary

1   In order to present the findings of an experiment, the data must first be organised, summarised and analysed.

2   Figures and tables that are included in the results section of a report must be referred to in the text. Any appendices should also be noted in the results section.

Before you move on to Session Ten, check that you have achieved the objectives given at the beginning of this session, and, if not, review the appropriate sections.

Experiment II: drawing conclusions

Introduction

In this session we will go through the process of interpreting the experiment and I shall then ask you to use that interpretation to prepare the discussion section of your report. The aim of the session is, therefore, to help you consolidate your understanding of how the features of the design and procedure can affect the interpretation of the results of an experiment.

Session objectives

When you have completed this session, you should be able to:

- interpret the results of a small-scale experiment
- draft the discussion section of an experimental report.

1: Interpreting the results

In Session Five we drew up a general plan for the process of interpreting an experiment. We will now make use of that plan to examine the meaning of the results that you have obtained.

As a reminder, the plan that we finally arrived at in section 2 of Session Five is reproduced as *Figure 7* below.

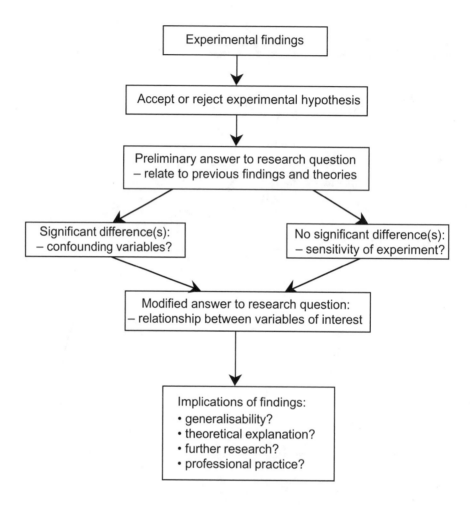

Figure 7 Plan for the process of interpreting an experiment

I intend to divide the process of interpretation into six separate steps simply to render it more manageable. Although this may make the exercise feel somewhat mechanical, once you have gained some experience of interpretation, you will be able to approach the task in a more flexible way. As I have pointed out previously, the approach we are going to use reflects my own views and is not intended to provide you with any absolute rules.

Experimental findings

At this point the findings that are reported in the results section should be stated and the important aspects emphasised. Given my findings, I would want to make it clear that no significant difference was obtained between the different delay conditions, although the mean recall scores do appear to decrease as the period between presentation and recall increases. I would also note the small decline in the percentage of items correctly recalled for each of the three conditions. Now have a try yourself.

ACTIVITY 39 — ALLOW 5 MINUTES

Write a few sentences describing your findings so that you bring out the important points. You can refer to any table or figure in the results section if this will help.

Commentary

These few sentences can form the opening to your discussion. They should give your reader a clear and unambiguous picture of the major findings of the study.

The fate of the experimental hypothesis

You can now turn your attention to the fate of the experimental hypothesis. Given my findings, I would have to state that the experimental hypothesis has received little support. The length of the delay between presentation and recall appears to have little effect on the level of forgetting. In other words, although the individuals tested only recalled less than half of the statements that they heard, immediate recall was little better than recall after an interval of an hour.

ACTIVITY 40 — ALLOW 5 MINUTES

Note down if your findings lead you to accept or reject the experimental hypothesis. Expand the statement a little as I have done above in order to make the outcome totally clear.

Commentary

You now have a very precise report of the findings of the experiment. We can use the information given so far to provide a preliminary answer to the research question and to consider how our findings relate to past studies or theories that were mentioned in the introduction.

A preliminary answer to the research question

My findings suggest that the length of the delay before recall has little effect on the forgetting of health-care-related information. In this respect they mirror closely the results reported by Ley (1972) and so lend support to the proposition that health care information is, for some reason, unusually resistant to forgetting.

Since a similar effect apparently occurs with both patients and healthy volunteers, the personal relevance of the information is unlikely to be the cause.

How do your findings relate to the research question and to the background material that you included in the introduction? Make a few notes on this subject now.

ACTIVITY 41 — ALLOW 10 MINUTES

Make some brief notes giving a preliminary answer to the research question and demonstrating how your findings relate to the previous work that you referred to in your introduction. You should look back to your introduction at this point to check the material that you covered and your original line of reasoning.

Commentary

You should be rather tentative in the conclusions that you draw at this point. You may have noticed that I used terms like 'suggest' and 'apparently'. This is because we are now going to look carefully at features of the design and procedure to try to assess the extent to which they may have contributed to the results. The preliminary answer to the research question may need to be modified in a number of ways.

Internal validity and sensitivity

It is at this point that you must focus steadily and consistently on the results that were actually obtained. You need to search for potential confounding variables if, and only if, you have a significant difference between treatment conditions. If there is no such difference, then there is little point in hunting for factors which might vary systematically with the independent variable.

My findings make it necessary to look for factors which might have decreased the sensitivity of the experiment. In Unit One we identified a number of features which contribute to the sensitivity of an experiment. They are as follows:

- control of extraneous variables
- magnitude of change in the independent variable
- measurement of the effects
- sample size.

In the current study, as we have already noted, the sample size was rather too small. This being the case, individual differences in memory ability between people may well have produced a degree of random error and so obscured the effects of the independent variable. Furthermore, the range of scores that could be obtained was very restricted. Thus, the measurement that we used was relatively insensitive and may not have been capable of detecting any effects. You may find this last point becomes clearer if you imagine that rather than scoring complete items recalled we had scored the number of words correctly remembered. Although such a score would have been inappropriate for our study, it might have detected differences in recall between the different delay periods.

You should now have a try at considering your data in a similar way.

Note down any features of the design or procedure that might account for the results you obtained. Refer to your notes of any observations that occurred to you while you were actually carrying out the study, or any comments that were made to you that may be of interest.

Commentary

Because our study was by no means perfect in terms of design, you will now probably want to modify the tentative conclusions that you drew previously. You can also begin to think about suggestions for further research which might test the experimental hypothesis more conclusively.

A modified answer to the research question

For both of the reasons given above, I would treat my findings with some caution and be unwilling to regard them as good evidence for the idea that there is something special about the forgetting of health-care-related information. The study would need to be replicated with a greater number of participants before any firm conclusions could be drawn.

External validity and implications

If, like me, you found no significant difference, you may feel that the results have no implications of any kind. This would not be true. I would want to point out that, although no general conclusions about the relationship between delay and forgetting can be drawn from this study, the findings do demonstrate clearly how much information is lost even with immediate recall, and so they support previous research.

The results from analogue studies with healthy volunteers cannot of course be generalised directly to clinical populations, and it may be that forgetting occurs for different reasons in patients and volunteers. Patients may fail to remember information because of stress and anxiety; volunteers because of a lack of personal relevance. This possibility could be tested by examining factors which might aid recall in the two different groups of people.

Now have a try at looking for the implications of your findings.

Note down any implications of your findings that you would want to bring out. Can you think of any other studies that could be carried out to examine the 'peculiarity' that Ley identified? Is the whole issue important in terms of its relevance to professional practice?

Commentary

You should now have a set of notes which can form the basis of your discussion. The aim of this section is to guide your interpretation of the experiment rather than to provide you with all the points that might be included in a discussion, so do not be surprised if some ideas have occurred to you which I have not mentioned. Include everything which seems relevant to you and then seek some feedback on your line of reasoning from your tutor.

2: Writing your research report – the discussion

You should now prepare a draft of the discussion section of your report.

ACTIVITY 44   ALLOW 45 MINUTES

Complete a first draft of the discussion section of the report. You can make use of the material provided above, but do check carefully that you have covered all the major points. You should also be sure to add a final paragraph which makes the conclusions clear.

Commentary

By this stage you have gained a considerable amount of experience of many aspects of experimental research. I realise that writing the report has been rather a long process, but I hope you appreciate that it will get easier and easier the more practice you have. It is worth getting a firm grip on the conventions of report writing. Once you feel certain about how to write, you will then be able to give your full attention to what to write.

Summary

1   The process of interpreting an experiment should be carried out in a highly structured way until the skill has been well practised.

2   The interpretation of an experiment must focus on providing possible explanations for the results that were actually obtained.

3   With practice, the skills of report writing become automatic and more attention can be paid to the quality of the content.

Before you move on to Session Eleven, check that you have achieved the objectives given at the beginning of this session, and, if not, review the appropriate sections.

Experiment II: preparing the report

Introduction

The purpose of this session is to enable you to add the remaining sections to your report and to produce a final, complete version. You will also be encouraged to use the checklist given in Session Six to take a critical look at the finished product. At the end of this session you should ask your tutor for feedback on the report. This process should help you to appreciate that it may be rather more difficult to evaluate your own work than it is to evaluate experimental research reported by other people.

Session objective

When you have completed this session, you should be able to:

- prepare a final draft of the whole of an experimental research report.

1: Completing the report

We have now reached the point of adding the final sections to your report. These are:

- title
- abstract
- references
- appendices.

The next activity will take you through the process of gathering together these sections.

ACTIVITY 45 ALLOW 30 MINUTES

Title

Using the format 'The effects of (independent variable) on (dependent variable)' write a title for your report. If there is any feature of the study that you want to draw attention to, you can put a colon and add it on the end.

Abstract

In no more than 200 words, write an abstract for the report you have drafted. If you found no significant difference, you should state that, because of flaws in the design and the small sample size, no firm conclusions can be drawn.

References

Check carefully through the draft of your report and make an alphabetically ordered list of any books or articles that you have cited. If you have read the original work, you should give the reference in the standard format. If you have not seen the original, then include the source of your information and use the form:

Bloggs, P. (1985), as cited in . . .

Appendices

Collect together your appendices which should consist of:

- instructions given to participants
- the raw data
- the calculations for the Kruskal-Wallis test.

These should be labelled Appendix 1, 2 and 3 respectively and included at the end of the report after the references.

Commentary

The report is now nearly complete. Just to remind you, the various sections should appear in the following order:

- title
- abstract
- introduction
- method
- results

- discussion
- references
- appendices.

Now you are ready to move on to preparing the final draft of your report.

2: Preparing a final draft

You should now be well prepared to produce a final draft of your report – I have no more words of advice or warning to offer!

ACTIVITY 46	ALLOW 90 MINUTES

Complete a final draft of your experimental report, being careful to use the appropriate style. A checklist was provided in Session Six which you might like to consult as you go along. Remember Clegg's (1982) advice that there are really only four vital questions to bear in mind:

- WHY?
- HOW?
- WHAT?
- SO WHAT?

Commentary

I hope that you are reasonably satisfied with the report that you have produced. You will have put in a great deal of hard work and effort to have reached this point, and you have every reason to feel pleased with your achievement.

You should now give or send your report to your tutor for comment.

3: Concluding comments

In the session that follows we will return to the issue of evaluating reports of experimental research, so this section concludes your experience of conducting research for this module. I want only to emphasise three important points.

First, be prepared for some aspects of your report to be challenged. There is no single correct way to present experimental research and your tutor may not agree with all the advice I have given you. You should not be too worried if this happens. Researchers often need to adopt slightly different conventions according to the audience. If you look at a range of published articles from different professional journals you will see that the presentation varies slightly from journal to journal. If, however, your tutor does not agree with your line of argument, then you will find it very valuable to discuss the point fully.

All of this leads me to stress yet again the importance of support and supervision from an experienced tutor. Although working through these units will have given you some very useful research experience, they should also have shown you the need for support and guidance when planning, conducting and interpreting experiments. I find that no matter how carefully I have considered a piece of research, colleagues can always add to and improve my ideas. Being able to observe and talk to participants is one of the advantages of the experimental approach, but it also has its drawbacks. You can be so convinced by the 'evidence' of your own eyes, that you fail to notice alternative explanations for your findings. An experienced supervisor will help you to look at your research with care and objectivity.

Finally, I hope that the studies we have carried out have convinced you of the need for replication. It is not only that some findings may fail to replicate for one reason or another, but that replication can provide important insights into the explanations that have been offered for particular sets of results. Only findings which are robust enough to be replicated, and which survive close critical scrutiny by other researchers, should form a basis for professional practice.

Summary

1   A complete practical report should consist of title, abstract, introduction, method, results, discussion, references and appendices in that order.

2   Researchers need to be flexible about some of the conventions of reporting research and adapt their method to their audience.

3   It is essential to have a period of supervision by an experienced tutor before embarking on independent research.

4   Replication of experimental research serves to check the reliability and generality of the original findings, and the explanation that was offered for them.

Before you move on to Session Twelve, check that you have achieved the objective given at the beginning of this session, and, if not, review the session as appropriate.

SESSION TWELVE

Evaluating experimental research

Introduction

The process of carrying out experimental research yourself should have increased your insight into some of the problems and possibilities. This should help you to appreciate the value of well-designed, careful experiments, and to identify when experimental evidence is not sound and why. In this session you will be asked to read and evaluate another report of some experimental research. Overall, the aim of the session is for you to practise and consolidate the skill that you have acquired in interpreting the results of experiments in the context of published experimental research.

Session objective

When you have completed this session, you should be able to:

- discuss and fully evaluate experimental research reports.

1: An experimental study - Todd, Reid and Robinson (1991)

As I have tried to emphasise throughout Units One and Two, the skills of evaluation and the skills of doing research are, to a great extent, two sides of the same coin. The more experimental research you design and carry out, the more familiar and comprehensible the logic of experimentation will seem to you. The more of your own experiments you attempt to interpret, the more obvious will the important features of any experiment appear. Similarly, the more you read and evaluate research by others, the more experience you will gain in dissecting experiments and the greater will be your understanding of the consequences of particular features of the design for the quality of the evidence that is obtained.

I suggest that you have another try now at reading and evaluating a published research article. You should find that your experience makes the task easier and more interesting than it may have seemed previously. An experimental study by Todd, Reid and Robinson (1991) is included as Resource 2 and it tackles the difficult question of the effects of the length of nursing shifts on patient care.

ACTIVITY 47　　　　　　　　ALLOW 45 MINUTES

Read carefully through the study by Todd, Reid and Robinson (1991) entitled 'The impact of 12-hour nursing shifts' which is included as Resource 2. Make a set of notes on the research that is reported.

Listed below are the headings we used for evaluation before:

- the research question
- the independent variable
- treatment conditions and people
- control
- measurement
- drawing conclusions.

You might like to make use of these headings again, but do not feel that you have to do so. Think, too, about whether you want to represent the design in diagrammatic form as we have done before.

Commentary

You might find it useful to get feedback from your tutor on your ideas. If you are working with other students, you could discuss your evaluations and the conclusions that you reach.

Here is my attempt with this article.

1　The research question

The research question arises not only from a concern about a current practical issue, but from a critical evaluation of the previous literature. In this way, the report provides a good example of how a careful appraisal of published research can lead to further research questions. The question that came early into my mind was about the measurement of the 'effects both on the care provided and on the nurses providing it'. It is not easy to translate concepts of this kind into dependent variables, so the issue of the reliability and validity of the measures is central. I also wondered about the possible impact of the observations and knowledge of the research project on the behaviour of the nursing staff involved.

2   The independent variable

The independent variable was the length of the nursing shift. As the researchers point out, not all of the differences between the two shift systems are reported in this paper. We have to assume that sufficient details have been included to interpret the findings that are presented. The research takes advantage of a naturally occurring change and is, therefore, not a true experiment. Because the effects of extraneous variables cannot be controlled in a natural experiment of this kind, it is not always easy to interpret any effects that are observed. One should, therefore, consider if there are any plausible alternative explanations, relating either to the people or to the situation.

3   Treatment conditions and people

Because measures were taken on the same wards before and after the change in shift length, the design is described as repeated-measures. But, clearly, the measures were not repeated on the same nursing staff or the same patients. This is an advantage in this case, since there can be no effect on the behaviour of the people concerned from repeating the measurement. It might have been interesting to know the extent of the staff changes between the two times when measurements were taken. It is, however, rather implausible to suggest that different staff and/or different patients could account for the results. The use of a large sample of wards helps in this respect. Diagrammatically, the design of the study is as follows.

	Stage 1	Stage 2
Condition 1 8-hour shift	Measures taken	
Condition 2 12-hour shift		Measures taken

The consent of the nursing staff or patients to the investigation is not mentioned, though it may be discussed in one of the other reports of the research. Since the 'cognitive functioning' of the staff was tested directly, it must be assumed that consent was obtained.

4   Control

No control of extraneous variables could be attempted in this study. It was noted, though, that the same total hours were worked for the two shift systems. Given the range of different wards, staff and patients, it is relatively unlikely that any factor varied systematically with the change in shift length. The number of extraneous variables would, however, introduce a high level of random error and so, potentially, reduce the sensitivity of the study. This might have made the interpretation of negative findings problematic – the sample size is important in this respect.

5   Measurement

The measures taken of patient care, nurses' attitudes and cognitive functioning seem careful. Although the quality of patient care is operationally defined, a range of different measures are used, rather than a simple arbitrary definition. The reliability and validity of all of the measures might have been mentioned. The different components of MONITOR are particularly important in this study because only some are sensitive to the change in shift length, although the effect is greater for some categories of patients.

The increase in non-care activities and decrease in direct nursing care also suggest that the nursing staff did not alter their behaviour because of the observations. The pattern of changes across the day tend to confirm that the change in shift length, rather than any other factor, is responsible for the overall effects.

6   Drawing conclusions

The summary of effects of twelve-hour shifts gives a very clear picture of the major findings. The researchers are also rightly tentative in some of the conclusions that they draw. For example, the behaviour of the nurses is attributed both to the shift system itself and to attitudes towards the system. It might be interesting to know, however, if positive attitudes towards twelve-hour shifts are related in any way to actual behaviour on the ward. Do the effects on quality of patient care occur regardless of the attitude of the individual nurse towards the shift length? Overall, the fact that not all of the detail could be included in this paper made a full evaluation rather difficult, but the findings and conclusions do seem clear.

How did you get on with this paper? I hope that you found that your knowledge of many of the basic concepts of experimental research helped to make the reading and evaluation of the published material easier to carry out. This was not, however, a simple paper to examine. We shall look at why this is the case and at one of the issues that it raised for me in the following section.

2: The purpose of evaluation

Evaluation and professional practice

I recently used the paper by Todd, Reid and Robinson (1991) with a group of health care students for an exercise in evaluation. The class was split up into small groups and asked to discuss the article with each other. After some time, I found that the groups looked rather depressed. When I asked why, one student said, 'I can't find anything wrong with it!' and the rest of the class nodded in gloomy agreement. This remark brought home very forcibly that we had not really tackled the whole issue of the purpose of evaluating research, and what to say about a paper which seems both sound and highly applicable.

Analysing series of articles can lead students to feel that the whole purpose is simply to find faults, rather than to evaluate in the fullest sense of the word. This is partly because when the exercise is conducted in something of a professional vacuum, little immediate use can be made of sound findings. Furthermore, there is no doubt that some published research is not as sound as it might be, and that the challenge of finding out what is wrong, and why, is an interesting and stimulating one. Going through an article and finding that everything seems as it should be can feel dull by comparison. But the challenge should never blind you to the fact that what is important is the search for good sound evidence on which to base professional practice.

Let's look at a recent article by Griffiths (1993) which makes a number of related points quite forcibly.

ACTIVITY 48   ALLOW **10** MINUTES

Read the article, 'To believe or not to believe' (Griffiths, 1993), which is included as Resource 3. Note the stress that he places on the value of reading original research articles and why the exercise is so crucial for health care practitioners.

Commentary

Many of the points that are made in the article will be familiar to you. Griffiths stresses that research findings cannot be translated into practice in any easy or mechanical fashion. He also brings out the purpose of evaluation – to guide and inform professional practice and so improve the care of patients and clients.

Formal critiques and professional practice

This being the case, you might like to have a look at an example of a critique of a nursing research paper as presented in a standard text on nursing research which is included as Resource 4.

ACTIVITY 49   ALLOW 20 MINUTES

Resource 4 is taken from Essentials of Nursing Research (Polit and Hungler, 1989). It is a very formal and thorough critique. Read through it carefully and note down any advantages and disadvantages that occur to you of critiques of this kind.

Commentary

Polit and Hungler give a very polished and careful performance. It is excellent as a model of the kind of points to look for in a research article. I believe, however, that it may also be misleading in some very important respects. When I started to teach research methods to health care students, I made use of similar critiques as models. What I found was that not only were people disappointed if they could not entirely dismantle an experiment, but that they could not in any way weight the criticisms that they made. I will explain what I mean by this below.

Writing very formal critiques of research articles can lead people to work rather rigidly and mechanically from the title to the references with careful comments on each section. At the end of the process, they can find it rather difficult to discriminate between the quality of the research and the quality of the research paper. There is, I believe, a crucial distinction between evaluating research papers and evaluating research. The difference lies in the weight that you accord to each feature of the paper. If you are a reviewer for a professional journal, you might give considerable weight to features such as the title and the abstract. If you are reading research to inform professional practice, then the important questions are the ones that Clegg (1982) listed:

- WHY?
- HOW?
- WHAT?
- SO WHAT?

Of these, the 'why' is probably the least important. The really critical features are what was done and what was found. You may, for example, remember the controversy over the survival rate of patients at the Bristol Cancer Help Centre (Bagenal *et al.* 1990) The original article showed a lower survival rate in patients attending the centre and receiving alternative therapies than in another group of patients receiving orthodox treatment at other hospitals. This finding was unfortunately used to comment on the efficacy of the therapies offered at the centre. Since, however, the researchers necessarily used a quasi-experimental design, there was no reason to assume that the two groups of patients were similar in relevant and important ways.

Thus, the meaning and application of research findings must be addressed through the questions:

- HOW was the research carried out?
- WHAT were the findings?
- SO WHAT conclusions can be drawn?

Evaluations of research articles should, I suggest, focus primarily on these questions and give real weight to aspects of the research article that provide the answers.

None of this should be taken to mean that the presentation of a paper is not important. If the presentation is very unclear then the content cannot be extracted. Rather, I am suggesting that in order to utilise research findings, close attention needs to be paid to the quality of the evidence presented. One of the dangers of lack of focus is that biases and personal prejudices may form part of the overall impression. Do you remember the paper by Hicks (1992) which was included as Resource 2 in Unit One? The research illustrates very clearly the way in which irrelevant features of an article, such as the gender of the author, can cloud the reader's judgement of the whole.

3: From evaluation to synthesis

If you approach the task of evaluation in the way that I have described above, I hope it will help you to combine the evidence from different research studies to give an overall picture. One of the problems that researchers can encounter is trying to reconcile conflicting findings. Brown, Meikle and Webb (1991) use an interesting approach to this problem, and you should have a look at their paper now.

ACTIVITY 50	ALLOW 20 MINUTES

Read carefully through the article by Brown, Meikle and Webb called 'Collecting midstream specimens of urine – the research base'. It is included as Resource 5. Do not worry if you are unclear about the analyses that they used, just note down your reactions to the approach. Can you see any advantages or disadvantages in the way in which they approached the problem of reconciling conflicting findings?

Commentary

The approach seems to me interesting though clearly quite time consuming. Essentially what the authors did was to analyse a large number of articles to see if the same variables had similar effects on bacterial contamination of specimens across different studies. As a first look at the literature this seems to be a useful and systematic exercise. You might, however, like to compare it with the approach taken by Todd, Reid and Robinson (1991) in their literature review. The advantage of the latter approach is that it synthesises the research through an evaluation of the quality of the evidence presented in the original articles. In the work of Brown, Meikle and Webb (1991) all the evidence is combined regardless of the way in which the research was carried out. As the authors note, any limitations of the original experiments will inevitably be transferred into their analyses.

In conclusion, a single important point emerges from this discussion. Research papers should be approached with a view to evaluating the quality and meaning of the evidence presented. This should help you not only to make sense of individual articles, but to combine the findings from different studies to gain an overall picture.

Summary

1   Evaluating and conducting experimental research can be seen as mutually supportive experiences.

2   The purpose of evaluating experimental research is to obtain sound evidence to guide professional practice. It is possible to lose sight of this objective.

3   A focus on the method and results of experiments helps to concentrate attention on the quality of the evidence. This is useful for evaluating individual articles and synthesising the findings from different studies.

Before you move on to Session Thirteen, check that you have achieved the objective given at the beginning of this session, and, if not, review the session as appropriate.

SESSION THIRTEEN

An overview of the experimental method

Introduction

In this final, brief session we shall return to our starting point and reconsider some of the criticisms of the experimental method. At the end of the session, you might like to go back and re-read Wilson-Barnett's defence of experiments which was included as *Resource 5* in Unit One.

Session objectives

When you have completed this session, you should be able to:

- describe the basis of the distinction between quantitative and qualitative research

- discuss the influence of a researcher's perspective on the research question posed and the research method adopted

- recognise the kind of questions that are best addressed by the quantitative method

- show an appreciation of the variety of different ways in which some research questions could be tackled.

1: Paradigms in health care research

Quantitative and qualitative research

In Session Seven of Unit One a distinction between qualitative and quantitative research was noted. At the time, I deliberately ducked most of the important issues and treated the distinction as meaning only whether findings are collected as 'numbers' or 'not numbers'. There are, however, considerably more fundamental differences between the two kinds of research, and the kind of data that is collected is only a symptom of underlying philosophical issues. In other words, 'qualitative' and 'quantitative' can be seen as representing two different research traditions. Since the experimental method is rooted very firmly in the 'quantitative' tradition, many of the criticisms of it are hard to understand without understanding the difference between the two traditions.

The following quotations should help to bring out some of the features of the essential difference between quantitative and qualitative approaches.

'The first view informs a quantitative approach to research and knowledge. That is, we view our patients objectively, as natural objects, and attempt to identify and measure important variables which represent the causes and expressions of a clinical condition . . . . The second view informs a qualitative approach to research and knowledge. We view our patients as persons and attempt to gain insights into their subjective experiences and the reasons for their actions in particular situations.'

(Polgar and Thomas, 1991)

'The word quantitative implies some form of measurement and is generally used to describe research studies in which an attempt has been made to measure research data in numerical terms. Qualitative research takes a different approach in that the researcher looks for "meaning".'

(Clifford and Gough, 1990)

'Quantitative research is concerned primarily with measurement of facts – about people, events or things – and establishing the strength of the relationship between variables, usually by statistics . . . . The theory behind quantitative research is that only by employing such methods can confidence be placed on the results and the hypothesis be adequately tested . . . . Qualitative research is based on the rationale that human behaviour can only be understood by getting to know the perspective and interpretation of events of the person or people being studied – by seeing things through their eyes – rather than by reliance on the measurement of concrete facts.'

(Couchman and Dawson, 1990)

ACTIVITY 51   ALLOW 5 MINUTES

Re-read the three quotations given above. Then place each of the following statements in either the 'quantitative' or the 'qualitative' tradition. You can do this by writing 'qual.' or 'quant.' against each one.

1   A researcher should choose a method of measurement that is as objective as possible.

2   It needs to be borne in mind that because people can make choices, they are essentially unpredictable.

3   It is essential to be able to generalise research findings from a sample to a population.

4   We cannot understand behaviour unless we also understand the meaning that the situation has for the person concerned.

Commentary

Statements 2 and 4 belong firmly in the qualitative tradition.

This activity may have helped to highlight the extent of the divide between the two approaches; in essence, they are based on very different models of what people are actually like. It is because of those implicit models that the different traditions favour and adopt different research approaches.

Positivism and phenomenology

The quantitative approach is based in a philosophical tradition known as **positivism**. Positivism represents a particular set of assumptions about the world and appropriate ways of studying it. It can, therefore, be described as a paradigm – a term that we met in Unit One. As McNeill (1990) explains:

Positivism: *essentially, the assumption that, given sufficient knowledge, all aspects of the world can be explained, predicted and controlled*

'[Positivists] assume that the natural world has an independent existence of its own, which is as it is regardless of those who are studying it, and which is governed by laws which can be discovered by the research scientist if only the right methods can be developed. The knowledge that is discovered using these methods is regarded as objective and factual, i.e. it is correct for all times and places.'

These assumptions are the basis of research in disciplines such as physics and chemistry. The quantitative approach uses similar methods with people because it regards the functioning of the social world as similar, in important respects, to the functioning of the natural or physical world.

The qualitative approach is associated with a rather different philosophical tradition known as **phenomenology**. Phenomenologists explicitly reject the use with people of an approach drawn from the natural sciences. They argue that any explanation of people must take into account what the people involved think and feel about the event or situation. There are, therefore, no laws governing the behaviour of people and no knowledge which will be correct for all times and places.

Phenomenology: *this contains the essential assumption that people are active and conscious and capable of making choices about how to act*

In essence, the quantitative approach can be characterised as a view 'from the outside', and the qualitative as a view 'from the inside'. Can you now see the relationship between the underlying philosophy and the kind of data collected? If people are viewed 'from the outside', then the data that are collected should be as concrete and objective as possible. Quantitative measures fit these requirements and can be analysed in various ways to bring out the similarities between individuals. If, by contrast, people are viewed 'from the inside' then it becomes essential to record their individual, subjective interpretations of situations and events.

The distinction between the quantitative and qualitative approaches is, therefore, considerably more fundamental than just the kind of data collected. The two approaches rest on very different sets of assumptions about the world, and so have different criteria for the selection and evaluation of evidence. They are, therefore, said to represent different paradigms.

On the face of it, the qualitative approach may sound like a more attractive option than the quantitative one. So stop for a few minutes and cast your mind back over the experimental research that has been described and that you have read while studying these two units. Does it still seem interesting and worthwhile? I hope so. There are, I believe, ways to reconcile the two paradigms which we will discuss in the last section of this session. Before we do, we need to reconsider the simple relationship which I outlined between research questions and choice of research method.

2: Choosing research methods

Throughout these two units I have emphasised the extent to which the research method that is adopted is determined by the nature of the research question. I have argued that experiments should be seen simply as the most direct, though certainly not the only, way to address predictive research questions. You may have begun to realise that matters are not quite as simple as that. The values of the researcher affect both the question that is posed and the kind of answer that is provided.

The best way to illustrate the issues is to take a typical 'predictive' research question; for example, 'Does the type of mattress used affect the development of pressure sores?'. Although researchers from both traditions might agree that this is an important question, it is one that is more likely to be addressed by someone working within the quantitative approach. Research questions are not in any sense neutral or value-free – they reflect the values of the researcher. People find certain things particularly interesting because they view the world in particular ways. Thus, the choice of the experimental method, and the choice of a research question which is best answered by the experimental method, are both partly determined by the values of the researcher.

Furthermore, some research questions can look very different according to the perspective from which they are viewed. Take for instance the example, 'Does routine weighing of pregnant women affect anxiety?'. From a quantitative perspective, this question would lead to a randomised controlled trial to examine the potential benefits and risks of routine weighing. From a qualitative perspective, it would be more likely to give rise to a study of how pregnant women make sense of the regular weighing and the meaning that they attribute to the event.

What is interesting about this is that both researchers would intend to offer an explanation of the effects of weighing. In quantitative research, explaining an event such as anxiety means identifying a cause of anxiety. In qualitative research, an explanation of anxiety involves discovering reasons for that anxiety. In other words, the two paradigms contain very different ideas about the nature of explanations. Thus, many 'predictive' research questions only lead to the use of the experimental method if an explanation in terms of causes is sought.

The following activity will encourage you to think a little more about this last point.

ACTIVITY 52   ALLOW **10** MINUTES

Look back to the paper by Todd, Reid and Robinson (1991) which is included as Resource 2. Note down for yourself how a researcher working in the qualitative tradition might approach the research question.

Commentary

Put simply, the research question that Todd, Reid and Robinson were addressing was, 'Does the length of the shift affect the quality of patient care?'. In their study, shift length was investigated as a cause of the behaviour of the staff towards the patients. A qualitative approach would have looked at what the change in shift length meant to the nursing staff and how their understanding of the situation affected their behaviour. In other words, it would have focused on the reasons why staff changed some aspects of patient care.

You may now be wondering if one of these approaches is intrinsically better than the other. I suggest not. It is important, though, to know exactly what information you will gain from doing an experiment. Only when you recognise what an experimental approach can tell you, can you use it in an appropriate way and recognise when it has been used appropriately. This point will be expanded in the section below.

3: Reconciling the paradigms

As I have presented the issues so far, it may seem to you that the two paradigms are diametrically opposed and that you are forced to make a permanent choice between them. My view may be rather simplistic, but I would suggest that there are two factors which make it possible for the different approaches to be reconciled.

First, there are different kinds of problems. The example we considered above relating to the effects of mattress type on pressure sores seems to me interesting and worthwhile and leads almost inevitably to the use of the experimental method. Many of the issues which are of concern from a qualitative perspective are simply not relevant to the problem. It is important to recognise times when this is the case. The quotation from Pulsford given below illustrates this point well. He refers to the paper by Brown, Meikle and Webb (1991) which you have read as *Resource 5* and states:

'The next 20 years of research into how to collect mid-stream urine specimens is no more likely to come up with a conclusion than the 30 years just gone. Nursing is about people and people, possessing infinite variety and – some would say – free will as well, are fundamentally inaccessible to science.'

(Pulsford, 1992)

Although people can exercise choice and although they are certainly unique in many important ways, these points seem scarcely relevant when considering how to avoid the contamination of urine samples. The thing to remember is that some problems can and should be addressed by the experimental method because there are no alternatives as powerful or informative.

The second factor to consider is that there are different aspects to the same problem. There is no reason to regard investigations of causes of events and investigations of reasons for people's actions as mutually exclusive. This point might have occurred to you during Activity 52. The two kinds of research would have complemented each other rather than conflicted – shift length could act as a cause of change in staff behaviour, but a different kind of understanding of the effects could be gained through a more qualitative approach.

Similarly, the problem investigated by Holden, Sagovsky and Cox (1989) which you read about during Unit One could be seen as having a number of different aspects. Although the article examined the effects of counselling by health visitors on postnatal depression, it did not tackle the issue of how health visitors, in the normal course of events, decide who is and who is not depressed. A qualitative study could look at this point.

Finally, it is worth bearing in mind that, although the experimental method is rooted in the quantitative tradition, it can to some extent be separated from it. As was emphasised in Unit One, it is perfectly possible to retain the essential core of the experimental method but to use qualitative instead of, or as well as, quantitative measurement. In this way, the effects of the deliberate introduction of change can be understood both 'from the outside' and 'from the inside'. As Wilson-Barnett concludes:

'This [experimental] approach can produce useful and powerful knowledge while respecting the rights of human subjects, who can also share their perspective with the researcher in a way which enriches the data and provides some benefits to those who make such research possible.'

(Wilson-Barnett, 1991)

The experimental method provides you with a powerful research tool. Like all other research methods, it should be used after careful consideration of the question that is being asked and the kind of answer that is required.

Summary

1   The distinction between quantitative and qualitative research rests on **philosophical issues** rather than the kind of data that are collected.

2   The choice of research question and research method reflects the values of the researcher.

3   Some research questions can only be addressed using a quantitative approach. Some research questions or topics might benefit from the use of both quantitative and qualitative techniques.

Now that you have completed the final session, check that you have achieved the objectives given at the beginning of this session, and, if not, review the appropriate sections. You can then go on to complete the Learning Review that follows this session.

LEARNING REVIEW

You can use the list of learning outcomes given below to review the progress you have made during this unit; the list is an exact repeat of the one provided at the beginning. You should tick the box on the scale that corresponds most closely to the point you feel you have achieved now, and then compare it with your scores on the learning profile you completed at the beginning of your study. If there are any areas that you are still unsure about, you might like to review the session concerned.

	Not at all	Partly	Quite well	Very well

Session One
I can:
- state when a research hypothesis is necessary ☐ ☐ ☐ ☐
- formulate an experimental hypothesis ☐ ☐ ☐ ☐
- outline the logic of hypothesis testing. ☐ ☐ ☐ ☐

Session Two
I can:
- identify sources of potential research questions ☐ ☐ ☐ ☐
- discuss how to approach the professional literature in a research context ☐ ☐ ☐ ☐
- outline the functions of the sections of a research report ☐ ☐ ☐ ☐
- describe the content and structure of the introductory section of a report. ☐ ☐ ☐ ☐

Session Three
I can:
- make decisions about the procedural details of an experiment ☐ ☐ ☐ ☐
- conduct an experimental procedure with precision ☐ ☐ ☐ ☐
- describe the content and structure of the method section of a report. ☐ ☐ ☐ ☐

Session Four
I can:
- explain the use of descriptive statistics to summarise the findings of an experiment ☐ ☐ ☐ ☐
- interpret the outcome of simple statistical tests ☐ ☐ ☐ ☐
- describe the content and structure of the results section of a report. ☐ ☐ ☐ ☐

	Not at all	Partly	Quite well	Very well

Session Five

I can:

- explain what the interpretation of an experiment involves ☐ ☐ ☐ ☐
- outline how to approach the process of interpretation ☐ ☐ ☐ ☐
- describe the content and structure of the discussion section of a report. ☐ ☐ ☐ ☐

Session Six

I can:

- write a title for a research report ☐ ☐ ☐ ☐
- write an abstract for a research report ☐ ☐ ☐ ☐
- describe the style in which a research report should be written ☐ ☐ ☐ ☐
- prepare a reference list for a research report. ☐ ☐ ☐ ☐

Session Seven

I can:

- describe how past research may generate new research questions ☐ ☐ ☐ ☐
- work out the procedural details for a small-scale experiment ☐ ☐ ☐ ☐
- write the introductory section of an experimental report. ☐ ☐ ☐ ☐

Session Eight

I can:

- conduct a small-scale experimental study ☐ ☐ ☐ ☐
- write the method section of an experimental report. ☐ ☐ ☐ ☐

Session Nine

I can:

- organise and summarise raw data from a small-scale experiment ☐ ☐ ☐ ☐
- select an appropriate statistical test for three or more treatment conditions and carry out the test using data collected ☐ ☐ ☐ ☐
- write the results section of an experimental report. ☐ ☐ ☐ ☐

Session Ten

I can:

- interpret the results of a small-scale experiment ☐ ☐ ☐ ☐
- write the discussion section of an experimental report. ☐ ☐ ☐ ☐

	Not at all	Partly	Quite well	Very well

Session Eleven

I can:

- prepare a complete report of a small-scale experiment ☐ ☐ ☐ ☐
- outline the main reasons for replication of previous experimental research. ☐ ☐ ☐ ☐

Session Twelve

I can:

- read and evaluate published reports of experimental research ☐ ☐ ☐ ☐
- evaluate experimental research to inform professional practice ☐ ☐ ☐ ☐
- synthesise findings from different experiments. ☐ ☐ ☐ ☐

Session Thirteen

I can:

- distinguish between different research paradigms ☐ ☐ ☐ ☐
- discuss how the paradigms might be reconciled ☐ ☐ ☐ ☐
- outline the most appropriate use of the experimental method. ☐ ☐ ☐ ☐

RESOURCES SECTION

Contents

RESOURCE I

*Clark, E. (1988)
Research Awareness,
Module 9: The
Experimental Perspective,
Section 7, pp. 34–44
(not SAQs)*

'There are lies, damned lies and statistics'

So far, I have discussed how researchers design their studies and gather their data, together with the validity of experimental research. We must now go on to consider how the data are analysed and the use of statistics to test hypotheses. This is often referred to as the **quantitative** analysis of data, as opposed to the qualitative type of data analysis referred to in Module 7: *The ethnographic perspective* and Module 8: *The survey perspective*.

I appreciate that the mere mention of the term 'statistics' is enough to make some people panic and feel totally inadequate, but please try to resist the temptation to skip the next few pages. You may rest assured that it is not my intention to turn you into a statistical expert overnight (that would require an entire course in its own right!). However, I do want to try to help you decipher the results sections of research reports and to understand the logic of hypothesis testing, together with the terminology that is used. In my experience, many nurses tend to skip this important section when reading a research paper.

The use of statistics in nursing is not new; Florence Nightingale was an able statistician. Palmer (1977) writes:
'Nightingale's reliance on statistics was based on the orderliness of her nature and her great attention to detail ... Her statistical evidence which could not be refuted was one reason why corrective reforms and actions were taken. Her statistical studies opened her eyes to the mortality of the British Army at home, in the Crimea, and in India. Convinced of the practical value of statistics, she used them to drive her messages home.'

However, at this point, you may be heartened to know that many people, researchers included, find statistics rather difficult, at least initially. In fact, many researchers seek help with the analysis of their data and also use computer packages such as the Statistical package for the Social Sciences (SPSSx). A computer can help in the analysis of data, but it will not interpret the outcome. It is, therefore, important for you to be able to understand how the result of a statistical test is used to test the original research hypothesis.

I need to introduce you to certain of the more important principles underlying the use of statistical tests. I hope to show you that the methods of establishing valid conclusions using statistics are both well-established and clearly defined. Although abuse is always a possibility, it is simply not the case that 'you can prove anything with statistics'. Nevertheless, statistics provide researchers with a powerful and necessary tool for analysing quantitative data and drawing valid conclusions from them.

Interpreting results

As we have already seen, the testing of hypotheses is at the heart of many research studies and all experimental research tests an hypothesis. The research hypothesis is formulated at the outset of the study, an appropriate research design is selected and the data are gathered. The next step is to interpret the results to see whether or not they support the prediction stated in the hypothesis at the outset.

But how does the researcher decide whether the data support the research hypothesis? How large do the observed differences between the conditions need to be in order to claim that the independent variable has produced a significant effect? It would be quite easy if all the subjects in one condition produced dramatically different scores from all the subjects in another condition. However, the outcome is rarely so straightforward - there is usually some degree of overlap between the scores for the different conditions which blurs the effects of the independent variable. For instance, a group of patients are allocated to one of two conditions: either an experimental group which is taught relaxation exercises pre operatively or a control group which is not. The post operative stress levels of patients in the two groups are later compared. Despite random allocation to conditions, some patients in the experimental group are likely to be very anxious and will score highly even though they have been taught how to relax, while others in the control group may naturally be very relaxed people and will score lower post operative stress levels than some of the patients in the experimental condition. Individual variation, therefore, usually ensures that there is considerable overlap between the measures of the dependent variable in the experimental and control conditions. You usually cannot say, just by looking at the data, that there is an obvious difference between the various conditions.

The results need, therefore, to be processed and analysed in some systematic way to find out whether the difference is sufficiently large for the researcher to feel reasonably confident that the manipulation of the independent variable was responsible for the observed outcome, rather than chance (or random) variation between the two groups.

A researcher does not want merely to report the scores of the different groups in the study (known as the **raw data**), but wants to use the data to test the original prediction as stated in the research hypothesis. This is the function of **inferential statistics**, which enable the researcher to draw inferences from the results of the research about the effects of the independent variable.

Statistical analysis is used to tell us whether or not the overlap between the scores of the different groups is too great to support the original prediction. It enables the researcher to calculate the probability of a specific set of results - to calculate the odds that the results of a particular experiment are merely due to chance (a fluke), rather than to the manipulated variable.

The researcher must, therefore, select and use an appropriate statistical test to analyse the raw data. You may be relieved to know that I do not intend to teach you how to do this for yourself, nor is it necessary for the nurse who is research-aware to master statistics! You only need to know that the choice of test depends on factors such as the kind of data to be analysed and the design of the study. In fact, selecting and using the right test is rather like knowing how to select and use the right tools to repair a car! If you are interested in pursuing this aspect further, there are a number of introductory textbooks and articles which explain these issues in more detail. I have listed some of the more readily available ones in Further Reading at the end of this module.

You do, however, need to be able to interpret the results reported in published research reports. In order to explain how hypotheses are tested, I must back-track for a moment and introduce another new concept. The logic behind hypothesis testing may seem rather awkward to you, at least initially. It is based on negative inference.

STATISTICIANS TAKE A NEGATIVE APPROACH

Null hypothesis

When the data are analysed statistically, the researcher begins by assuming that the different sets of data, collected under the various conditions of the experiment, do not differ. Whatever the independent variable, it is assumed at the outset not to have produced the effect on the dependent variable that was predicted by the research hypothesis. This statement of no difference, or no relationship, between the variables is known as the **null hypothesis**. The null hypothesis, therefore, states the possibility that the results of the experiment are due to chance fluctuations in subjects' behaviour rather than to the predicted effects of the manipulated variable. A scientist can never directly prove that the research hypothesis is correct but can, however, show that the null hypothesis has a high probability of being incorrect. It is, therefore, the null hypothesis which is directly tested - and not the research hypothesis.

Think back to the study by Boore (1978) in which she investigated the effects of the pre operative preparation of surgical patients on post operative stress, recovery and infection. One of the hypotheses that she tested was:

'The pre operative giving of information about prospective treatment and care, and the teaching of exercises to be performed post operatively, will minimise the rise in biochemical indicators of stress.'

There are two possible outcomes: either the suggested treatment produces an effect - or it does not, in which case any differences would not be due to the treatment, but to chance variation. Now the first of these two alternative outcomes is always stated within the research hypothesis. If you are uncertain about this, then taken another careful look at Boore's hypothesis above.

The second possible outcome is the null hypothesis (sometimes referred to as the statistical hypothesis). The null hypothesis is quite simply a statement that there is no relationship between the variables and that any observed differences are only due to chance variation. The null hypothesis would simply state that both the giving of information pre operatively and the teaching of exercises to be performed post operatively will not produce any effects on biochemical indicators of stress. It is a statement predicting that the independent variable will have no effect on the dependent variables - that there will be no difference between the levels of stress experienced by the experimental group who receive the treatment and the control group who do not.

The next activity will look at another example to provide some practice in recognising a null hypothesis.

Activity 9.15   *Allow 5 minutes*

In her evaluation of health visitor intervention with elderly women, Luker (1982) posed two research hypotheses and two null hypotheses which are quoted below. Read each one carefully and identify the two research hypotheses and the two null hypotheses.

1   That there is no significant difference in the number of health problems which improve in elderly women aged 70 years and over, who live alone, at home, after focused health visitor intervention once monthly for four months.

2   That there is a significant difference in the number of health problems which improve in elderly women aged 70 years and over, who live alone, at home, after focused health visitor intervention once monthly for four months.

3   That there is no significant difference in the life satisfaction score on the LSI-A [Life Satisfaction Index-A] in women aged 70 years and over, who live alone, at home, after focused health visitor intervention once monthly for four months.

4   That there is a significant difference in the life satisfaction score on the LSI-A in women aged 70 years and over, who live alone, at home, after focused health visitor intervention once monthly for four months.'

Commentary

I hope that you were able to recognise 2 and 4 as the research hypotheses and 1 and 3 as the null hypotheses. The null hypotheses both predict that there are no significant effects of the independent variable (in this case, focused health visitor intervention once monthly for four months) on the dependent variables (number of health problems in Hypothesis 1 and life satisfaction score as measured by the LSI-A in Hypothesis 3).

The research hypothesis is sometimes referred to as Hi and the null hypothesis as Ho. You may come across this notation in your reading, but try not to let it put you off. You will find when reading a research study in which an hypothesis is tested that the research hypothesis will always be clearly stated (or should be!), but that the null hypothesis may not be. Not all researchers list their hypotheses as clearly as Luker.

However, whether it is stated or not, the null hypothesis always makes a crucial contribution to the logic behind the testing of hypotheses. From the outset, the null hypothesis is assumed to be true and the researcher must gather evidence to dis-prove it, in which case the results will support the research hypotheses.

But before I go on to describe how the null hypothesis is tested, I need to briefly revise your understanding of probability - a concept familiar to all of us in our everyday lives, as the following short activity will demonstrate.

Activity 9.16   *Allow 5 minutes*

Using a scale of 0 (impossibility or no chance of something occurring) to 100 (absolute certainty), estimate the likelihood of the statements listed below. Record your answers in the boxes.

For example, whenever I go into college, there is a strong chance that I will meet my head of department, and so I give this a score of 85, but it is highly unlikely that I will meet the director of the college and so I give this a score of only 8.

What is the likelihood of:

(a) Getting the 'heads' side on a single coin tossed once? ☐

(b) You being made redundant? ☐

(c) You taking a patient's temperature during your next span of duty? ☐

(d) You reading a research paper within the coming week? ☐

(e) You catching a red bus during the next month? ☐

(f) You flying by Concorde to New York? ☐

When you have done this, mark the position of each of your estimates on the scale below:

```
0              50          100
|__|__|__|__|__|__|__|__|__|__|
```

Commentary

Your answer to (a) should be 50. Your other estimates will obviously reflect your own particular situation. For me, (d) is the most likely (scoring 98) and (f) is the most unlikely (scoring 3).

When statisticians refer to the concept of probability (which is usually indicated by the symbol p), they express it numerically on a scale of 0 to 1, where 0 represents no chance of something occurring and where 1 means that it is certain to occur. Using this scale, a probability of 5 out of 100 would be written as 0.05, 10 our of 100 as 0.1, 50 out of 100 as 0.5 and so on. The probability of my dying, or anyone else for that matter, is 1. However, the probability of my dying within the next five years is (I hope!) considerably less, say 0.05.

In *Figure 1*, I have plotted a number of known probabilities on a probability scale.

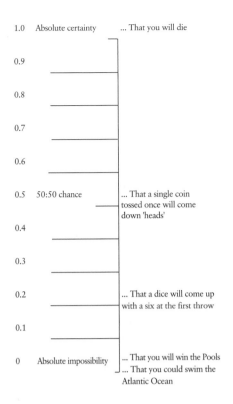

Figure 1 The probability scale

The next activity is intended to ensure that you are thoroughly familiar with this scale of probabilities, since it is the notation that you will find when reading research reports.

Activity 9.17   *Allow 5 minutes*

1 Using the scale of 0 to 1, estimate the probability of a pregnant woman having a baby girl.
2 Now go back to your estimates of the likelihood of events in Activity 9.16. Translate each one onto the scale of 0 to 1 and add it to the probability scale in *Figure 1*.

Commentary

1 The probability of a pregnant women having a baby girl is 0.5.
2 Returning to my own earlier estimates, the probability of (d) would be 0.98 and the probability of (f) would be 0.03.

Statistical significance

Understanding the concept of probability is crucial to understanding the principles of hypothesis testing. A statistical test is simply a means of calculating the likelihood, or probability, that the results are due to random fluctuations between the conditions. Thus, it is the null hypothesis that is actually being tested. If it is very *unlikely* that the difference could have been caused by chance - say a probability of 1 in 100 (or 0.01) - then the researcher can feel more confident that there is a *real* difference between the conditions as a

result of the manipulation of the independent variable. The difference is then said to be **statistically significant**, and the results support the research hypothesis. In other words, the less likely that a particular difference in scores can be said to have happened purely by chance, the more confident the researcher can feel that it is a real predicted difference. If, on the other hand, the probability that the results could have occurred by chance is much higher, then there is no reason to assume that they were due to the effects of the independent variable; the findings are then said to be non-significant. A **non-significant** outcome means that the results can be explained by random, or chance, fluctuation. It is, therefore, the probability value of any test statistic that is used as a basis for accepting or rejecting the null hypothesis, and hence the research hypothesis.

Naturally, most researchers hope for significant results since these are necessary to support the original prediction in the research hypothesis. The term 'significant' in the context of research findings is used in a statistical sense, based on the probability of a particular set of results occurring by chance alone. Statistical significance does not mean 'important' or 'meaningful', and must not be confused with clinical significance. A difference between two groups of patients which is statistically 'significant' may not be of any great interest or importance in a clinical sense. Barlow, Hayes and Nelson (1984) provide a good illustration of this point:
'If anxiety were reliably measured on a 0 to 100 scale, with 100 representing severe anxiety, a treatment that improved each client in a group of anxiety neurotics from 80 to 75 would be statistically significant if all anxiety neurotics in the control group remained at 80. But this improvement would be of little use to the clinician, since the clients in the treatment group would probably not notice the improvement themselves and would certainly still be very anxious. An improvement of 40 or 50 points might be necessary before both the clinician and the client considered the change clinically important.'
The term 'significant' in the context of statistical analysis of data must not mislead you. It simply means that the observed difference or relationship between the scores is statistically signifi-

cant. Statistically significant findings don't necessarily imply that others will be able to perceive a real change or difference. It is particularly important to remember this when reading about, or participating in, clinical trials; in addition to a statistically significant improvement in outcome, any new treatment tested in a randomised controlled trial must also produce changes which are of clinical significance.

You may have spotted that there is just one difficulty left - just how unlikely must the chance explanation be before we reject it, regard the results as significant and accept the research hypothesis? The researcher sets a **significant level** at the outset and uses this as the cut-off point. It is essentially an arbitrary matter rather than a basic principle. Many researchers adopt a significant level of 0.05 (a 5 in 100 chance) which means that the difference between groups will be assumed to reflect chance variation unless the results could only arise by chance 5 times in 100, or less. Thus, the chance explanation (the null hypothesis) is only rejected when it is highly improbable: 0.05 is the highest level of probability which it is usual to accept as statistically significant.

Statistical significance tends to baffle people, but briefly all it means is this: the researcher has found a difference between two samples which have been treated in different ways. If twenty pairs of samples were selected from a very large number of individuals with no regard for how they had been treated, one would get a difference of this size once (or less) purely on the grounds of chance variation. That is to say, the probability of finding a difference as great as this between two groups of subjects by chance variation is only 1 in 20 or 5 times in 100.

We have covered a lot of ground and I have introduced a number of new concepts over the last few pages. I will now summarise the whole process of statistical inference and hypothesis testing for you:

1 The research hypothesis should always be clearly stated. The null hypothesis may not be stated, but it is still crucial since it predicts that the manipulation of the independent variable does not affect the outcome of the study. It is the null hypothesis which is actually tested.

2 The significance level is set at the outset by the researcher.

3 An appropriate statistical test is selected (depending on the design of the study) and carried out on the data to calculate the probability (p) that the results could have been obtained by chance variation alone: i.e. the probability of the null hypothesis being the correct explanation of the findings.

4 The null hypothesis is accepted if the probability value is greater than the significance level. If the latter is set at 0.05, the null hypothesis is accepted if the probability of the results occurring by chance variation is greater than 0.05. This is often written as $p > 0.05$. In this instance, the researcher is claiming that he or she does not have sufficient evidence to reject the null hypothesis. If the null hypothesis is accepted then the research hypothesis, which represents the alternative explanation, must be rejected.

5 The null hypothesis is rejected if the probability of the results is less than or equal to the significance level ($p \leq 0.05$), in which case the alternative hypothesis - the research hypothesis - is accepted. The researcher may then claim that the difference between the groups is significant and can be attributed to the independent variable. You need to remember that the research and null hypothesis are alternative explanations of the outcome of a study: either the null hypothesis is accepted and the research hypothesis is rejected, or the null hypothesis is rejected and the research hypothesis is accepted (see *Figure 2*).

If the probability of a particular set of results occurring by chance is *greater than* the significance level, the researcher accepts the *null hypothesis* (Ho) and *rejects* the *research hypothesis* (Hi). Thus, if the calculated probability of a particular set of results lies to the right of the vertical line indicating the significance level (see *Figure 2*), the null hypothesis must be accepted. If, however, the probability is less than or equal to the significance level then the researcher will reject the null hypothesis (Ho) and accept the research hypothesis (Hi). This is indicated in *Figure 2* by the region immediately to the left of the vertical line indicating the significance level. Note: in this figure, the significance level has been set at 0.05.

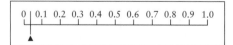

Figure 2 Probability scale with significance level set at 0.05.

You will probably need to read through these points several times to be sure that you have understood the logic of the process. Many students find these ideas particularly difficult because they feel that they are the opposite of what they would expect. You must understand that the effects of the independent variable are not tested directly but by dismissing the possibility, based on probability, that they were produced by chance variation. Note the notation that I have introduced which is commonly used in research reports:

< meaning less than
≤ meaning less than or equal to
> meaning greater than
≥ meaning greater than or equal to.

If you have followed the logic of hypothesis testing, you will probably realise that we can never be absolutely certain about a decision based on statistics. If the null hypothesis is rejected whenever the probability of the results falls below 0.05, the correct decision will be made most of the time. Occasionally, however, the null hypothesis will be rejected when it is, in fact, correct. The probability of committing such an error is equal to the significance level selected: that is, if the latter is set at 0.05 (or 5 per cent) then the experimenter would be wrong five per cent of the time, which is considered by most researchers to be an acceptable margin of error. The likelihood of making this kind of 'mistake' can, however, be reduced by reducing the level of significance to say, 0.01 (or 1 per cent). Some researchers, therefore, set a more stringent 'cut-off' point of 0.01 (a 1 per cent chance). If the significance level is set at 0.01 then the cut-off point would be moved even closer to 0; you might like to mark it on *Figure 2*.

If you find this idea of the researcher making a 'mistake' difficult to grasp, then the following example might help. Suppose you are tossing a coin over and over again. There would be a high probability that you would tend to get equal numbers of heads and tails (you could try this if you like). Let us suppose that you actually did this and that you got heads every time on ten tosses. You might well conclude that the coin was biased towards heads and that the tosses were not, therefore, random. However, you should overlook the very, very small probability that a run of ten heads in a row could occur solely by chance (and may help to explain why people gamble at casinos!). This example illustrates that even highly significant differences in results between the groups of a research study could occur by chance alone and might not be due to the manipulated variable, and that the risk of this happening is equal to the significance level. To further reduce this risk, the significance level would need to be shifted even closer to 0, and may be set at 0.01.

It must be emphasised at this point that hypotheses can never be ultimately proven through hypothesis testing. A researcher should, therefore, never claim that his or her findings proved that an hypothesis, or a theory, was right. Research findings can only support an hypothesis and should always be considered tentative. This is obviously an important issue when it comes to applying research findings in professional practice. We see, in Module 11: *Using research findings in nursing care*, how important it is for studies to be replicated. Only when similar results are produced by different studies can greater confidence be placed in the conclusions. Hypotheses and theories can only come to be increasingly believed or accepted with accumulating evidence, but their validity can never be ultimately proven. Scientists can never know that any of their theories are true; for instance:

'The overthrow of Newtonian explanations ... provided a striking case of a theory, which had been confirmed countless times and in very many different areas, finally falling foul of observational counter-evidence. In the end, its incredible success over 200 years counted for nothing: it was false'.

(O'Hear, 1985)

Newton believed that the length of a rigid object appeared to be constant, whether it was moving or not, relative to an observer (an absolute notion of length). However, Einstein subsequently showed that a rigid object moving past an observer appeared, to the observer, to be shorter than the same object when stationary (a relative notion of length). This lack of absolute validity - this 'relativity' to a particular observer - is a property shared by other physical quantities, including mass and time. Thus, the most elementary physical measurements - those of mass, length and time - are found to be relative to a particular observer and nobody can state, absolutely, what their values are.

Statistical analysis

There are many different statistical tests which a researcher can use to analyse data and test for statistical significance. Each test has a name: for instance, the t-test, the chi-squared test and the Mann-Whitney test. The researcher selects a test that is appropriate to the design of the study and the type of data collected, and should specify which test is used. This test is then used to analyse the data and to calculate the precise value of the test statistic (for example, 't' in the case of the t-test, 'X2' in the case of the chi-squared test and 'U' in the case of the Mann-Whitney test). This value must then be looked up in the appropriate statistical tables to find out the probability of those particular results occurring by chance. This enables the researcher to discover the exact probability of getting the results by chance alone (that is, the probability of the null hypothesis being accepted). It is the probability value, rather than the value of the test statistic itself, which is important and which enables a decision to be made about whether or not the results are significant and whether the null hypothesis is accepted or rejected. Remember, the probability value needs to be very small (depending on the level of significance chosen) for the results to be statistically significant and support the research hypothesis and not, as many people imagine, the other way round. An hypothetical example and extracts from the results sections of two research papers, which we will look at later in this section, should help to further clarify your understanding of the statistical analysis of quantitative data.

If you have read Module 5: *Identifying and defining questions for research,* you may remember that a research hypothesis can be either one-tailed (directional) or two-tailed (non-directional). The type of hypothesis to be tested has implications for statistical analysis and affects the probabilities that the differences will occur by chance. There is a specific probability that the difference will occur by chance for an hypothesis which predicts a difference in one direction only. If, however, an hypothesis makes a prediction that a difference might occur in either direction, then the probability that the differences will occur by chance is doubled. The researcher will, therefore, take this into account when looking up the probability of a test statistic and will usually report whether a one or two-tailed test was used. For the present, you only need to know that this decision depends on the wording of the original hypothesis - a one-tailed test is used with a one-tailed hypothesis and a two-tailed test with a two-tailed hypothesis.

To illustrate the stages of hypothesis testing using statistical analysis, I will take you through an hypothetical experimental study of the benefits of introducing a token economy programme in a unit for moderately mentally handicapped adoles-

cents. The one-tailed research hypothesis predicts that the introduction of a token economy programme (the independent variable) will reduce the incidence of anti-social behaviour (the dependent variable). Using a between-subjects design, the researcher randomly allocates ten of the twenty clients resident in the unit to an experimental group while the remaining ten individuals act as a control group. The researcher starts by observing and recording the existing behaviour patterns of all the residents over a period of seven consecutive days (the baseline or pre-test) and then introduces a token economy programme in the experimental group.

At the end of two months, the researcher again records the behaviour patterns of all the clients for seven consecutive days (the post-test). The results show a small overall reduction in the incidence of anti-social behaviour for the experimental group while little change is observed in the control group. However, behaviour patterns have differed within each of the two groups, and there is a considerable overlap between them, as shown in *Table 2*. Incidentally, the dependent variable - the number of anti-social incidents - would need to be operationally defined by the researcher (see Module 5: *Identifying and defining questions for research*) in order that the results should be objective.

Experimental group token economy programme (n = 10)			Control group (n = 10)		
Subject	Pre-test	Post-test	Subject	Pre-test	Post-test
S1	15	13	S11	8	10
S2	7	5	S12	12	12
S3	9	9	S13	2	3
S4	9	6	S14	14	12
S5	5	5	S15	12	15
S6	8	7	S16	10	13
S7	11	7	S17	9	12
S8	10	8	S18	16	13
S9	12	10	S19	7	9
S10	4	3	S20	6	5
Mean:	9.0	7.3	Mean:	9.6	10.4

Table 2 Number of anti-social incidents recorded over seven consecutive 24-hour periods

The significance level is set at 0.05. A number of different statistical analyses are possible using these data. For instance, the researcher might decide to analyse the post-test scores for the two groups using the Mann-Whitney test (the appropriate statistical test for a between-subjects comparison involving two conditions). When she does this she finds that the incidence of anti-social behaviour is significantly less in the experimental group (using the token economy programme) than in the control group (U - 25.5, p< 0.05, one-tailed test). Consequently, the null hypothesis can be rejected and the research hypothesis accepted. The results support the prediction that the introduction of a token economy programme will reduce the incidence of anti-social behaviour observed in a unit for moderately mentally handicapped adolescents.

In this hypothetical example, I have introduced you to the kind of notation you are likely to encounter when reading an experimental report. I hope you didn't find it too confusing! Let me talk you through it once more:

- The researcher is using the Mann-Whitney test to analyse the data - in this example, the differences between the post-test scores for the two different conditions (experimental and control).
- The test statistic for the Mann-Whitney test is U.
- The value for U as calculated using the Mann-Whitney test is 25.5.
- The probability of this specific value

for U is less than 0.05 (using a one-tailed test because the original research hypothesis is one-tailed); this means that the probability of these results occurring by random variation or chance is less than 5 per cent (less than 5 in 100).

- Since the probability is less than the significance level (which was set at 0.05), the null hypothesis can be rejected.
- If the null hypothesis is rejected, the research hypothesis must be accepted - the results are said to be statistically significant - and the results support the prediction made by the research hypothesis.

Remember, it is the reported probability of the results which determines whether or not the results are significant. If the probability is greater than the significance level, the null hypothesis is accepted and the research hypothesis rejected; if it is smaller than, or equal to, the significance level, the null hypothesis is rejected and the research hypothesis is, therefore accepted.

The impact of 12-hour nursing shifts

RESOURCE 2

Todd, C., Reid, N. and Robinson, G. (1991), Nursing Times, 87 (31), July 31, pp. 47-50.

This paper reports on the findings of a study to test the effect of a 12-hour shift system on the provision of nursing services. It was shown that, in comparison with the more traditional eight-hour shifts, overall there was little justification for introducing shifts of 12 hours. First, a brief review of the literature which formed the background to the study is given.

Over recent years, NHS managers have been under increasing pressure to improve the cost-effectiveness of services. Some health authorities have shown interest in introducing 12-hour nursing shifts with a view to the reduction of the overlap between shifts and the potential financial savings which may ensue. Such changes in working practices could have major effects on the services provided.

Background literature

A number of previous papers on 12-hour shift systems have reported benefits such as positive attitudes of staff about travel to work and time off duty (1); improved quality of patient care and enthusiasm among staff (2); benefits to staff education (3) and improved staff morale and reductions in absenteeism rates (4 5). Others, while reporting no detrimental effect on job satisfaction or opinions from doctors about nursing services, claim there are some benefits, since the majority of nurses favour a 12-hour shift (6). But other researchers have pub-

lished less favourable reports on the subject, with reduced quality of care (7) and dislike of the shift among the nurses working it (8) being identified as major problems.

Johnston *et al.*(9) reported lowered cognitive performance in nurses working 12-hour shifts, such that they had higher error rates at the beginning of the day on tasks requiring vigilance and those where their reaction time is important.

A number of studies report both positive and negative effects of 12-hour shifts. One concluded that benefits in job satisfaction and the organisation and delivery of care were outweighed by fatigue and disruption of nurses' family and social lives (10). But another reported that while staff initially were in favour of the shift, their satisfaction declined with further experience of the shift (11).

These authors, however, report no difference in patient satisfaction, nor in the standard of nursing care under 12-hour shifts (11). Other authors also report no changes in quality of care, (but apparent reductions in the continuity of care (12)), or no changes in nurses' job satisfaction and reported fatigue and health (13). It has been pointed out that the mode of implementation of the shift system may be a crucial factor in whether or not it is successful (14).

To date, research into the 12-hour shift system has been conducted predominantly in the United States and Canada, typically on a small scale (one or two wards) and in urban locations. The majority of the studies involved nurses who had opted voluntarily to work a 12-hour shift on a relatively short-term experimental basis and thus may have been biased in favour of the shift. Furthermore, in all cases the studies reviewed suffer from methodological flaws. In some cases the authors fail to report any data which support the assertions made. Sometimes it appears that authors give their personal impressions of shift systems rather than offering scientific evidence. Furthermore, some authors have not always been as critical and rigorous in reviewing the literature as they might have been, so that without reading the original papers it is possible to be misled.

In overview, when a rigorous evaluation of the scientific evidence is made, the conclusions that can be validly drawn from the literature are limited. What is abundantly clear, however, is that changes in nursing shifts could have important effects on both the care provided and on the nurses providing it.

The study

We were commissioned by one health board to evaluate the 12-hour shift which was being introduced into all in-patient units in the board's area. Under this type of shift, nurses work on average three-and-a-half days a week, as opposed to the more traditional eight-hour shifts worked, on average, five day a week. Under both systems, full-time nurses worked the same total hours: 75 hours a fortnight.

The study was the first full-scale evaluation of the shift in the UK and comprised repeated measures (before and six months after) on 10 in-patient wards in two hospitals, situated in the county town of a rural area. These hospitals were chosen because they were the only ones in which the 12-hour shift was not being worked in the health board at the time the study was begun. The repeated measures design enabled us to collect data on the wards before the introduction of a 12-hour shift, permitting direct inferences to be made about the effect of the shift in the same wards.

Our study was designed to investigate the effect of the 12-hour shift on: patient care in terms of both the quality and quantity of care provided; nurses' attitudes towards their work and their cognitive functioning during the shift.

This paper gives an overview of the most important findings, but does not report every difference between the two shift systems. Further details on methodology and findings can be found elsewhere (15-22).

Patient care

The quality of patient care was evaluated using MONITOR, an index of the quality of care based on the nursing process (23, 24). The quality of care provided under the 12-hour shift system was statistically significantly poorer than that provided under the eight-hour shift, with a mean decrease of 11% for the total MONITOR score (17). The 12-hour shift scores were significantly poorer for the components of quality representing the planning of care (-12%), catering for patients' psycho-social needs (-9%) and evaluation of nursing care objectives (-14%). For the delivery of physical care there was no statistically significant difference between the two shift systems, although the observed decrement (-6%) did approach significance. As one might expect there was no difference between the scores the two shift systems received on the 'Ward Monitor' scale, since the wards were essentially the same physically and organisationally under both shift systems.

The changes in the quality of care for different dependence groups of patients was also considered using Hospital Systems Study Group (HSSG) dependency classifications (25). While the overall quality of care for all dependency groups dropped, it was the higher dependency patients who were most adversely affected, especially in terms of the physical and psycho-social care provided (17).

The quantity of patient care was measured using 'activity analysis'. This is a behavioural analysis of nurses' activity which gives a classification of observations under four super-ordinate categories of behaviours: direct nursing care (hands-on care); indirect care (preparation, planning, clerical and administrative); routine care (hotel and catering-type activities); and non-care activities (meal breaks and unofficial breaks) (15, 19).

An important difference between the two shifts was the drop in time spent by nurses on the direct care of patients. This went down from being 46% of observations to 39.7%, even when the differences

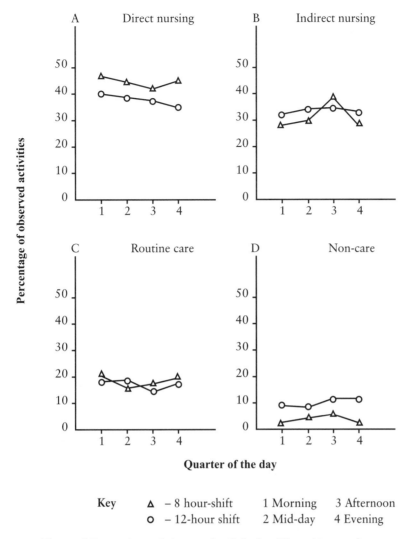

Figure 1 Percentage of observed activity for different types of care.
Data exclude official meal breaks

in meal breaks between the shift systems had been allowed for. This drop was complemented by an increase in non-care activities (excluding official breaks). The amount of time spent on indirect care and routine care remained the same for both shifts. This pattern was statistically significant and consistent across wards.

The pattern of activities during the day also changed. This was characterised by a reduction in the amount of direct nursing care from the early morning to the late afternoon (*Figure 1*). Under the 12-hour shift the decline continues and direct care is least prevalent during the early evening. But under the eight-hour shift the amount of direct care picks up again in the early evening to reach an overall daily peak. Indirect nursing activities remain basically stable throughout the day under the 12-hour shift, but under the eight-hour shift peak in the afternoon, probably reflecting the handovers that occur then. Non-care activities are higher throughout the day under the 12-hour shift and the disparity

between the two shifts becomes greatest at the end of the day.

We interpreted these data in terms of a pacing effect: nurses who know they are going to be on duty all day results in their pacing their work from the very beginning. It is also worth noting that the lack of difference between shifts for the amount of indirect care performed runs counter to the rationale for the introduction of the longer shifts as a way to reduce the overlap between shifts (*19*).

Nurse education

We considered the effects of the shift on nurse education in a number of ways. The most objective (because it is behavioural rather than report-based) and thus convincing evidence concerning the effect of the shift on education is to be found among the activity analysis data. Most important are the working combinations of the nurses observed. These changed between the two shift systems (*20*).

Overall, some two-thirds of activities

undertaken in the wards were carried out by a single nurse working on her own, while a quarter were carried out in pairs of nurses and not quite 10% by nurses working in combinations of three or more. There was, however, a small but significant increase under the 12-hour shift in the amount of work done by nurses in pairs. Given the apprenticeship model of nurse training this could have been advantageous to training. Unfortunately this does not appear to have been the case. Rather than working with and supervising students, the trained nurses were observed to be working more often with auxiliaries under the 12-hour shift while students worked more with each other. There was also a dramatic drop in the percentage of occasions when staff nurses and students were paired for situations which were observed to be overtly educational (from 50% to 17%).

This is another finding which has a time of day specificity. There were very different patterns between the two shifts and the lowest levels of education were found on the afternoons and evenings of the 12-hour shift. Also, when we analysed the amount of time spent by students with patients of different dependencies, we found significant differences between the two shift systems. Much of this difference appears to result from the finding that the students spent less time in direct contact with patients under the 12-hour shift system *(20)*. Thus student nurses had less experience of performing nursing procedures and less supervision by trained nurses.

Nurse educators and students were surveyed about their views on the effects of the shift system *(21)*. Nurse educators were almost unanimous in their condemnation of the 12-hour shift system, feeling it made for organisational difficulties, as well as being detrimental to the education process *per se*. The student nurses, on the other hand, were reasonably positive towards the 12-hour shift; in fact they were more positive as a group than any other cross-section of nurses surveyed. It appears that this attitude related to perceived social rather than professional benefits. As the students were generally young and single, the long blocks of off-duty, which the 12-hour shift engendered, were an attractive feature for them.

Patient views

Questionnaires were distributed to patients in the wards of the two study hospitals *(15)*. We interviewed those who could not complete it or needed help in doing so. Some patients preferred not to take part in the study. Completed questionnaires or interviews were obtained from 143 patients.

There were very few differences in patients' views between the two shift systems. Some 92% of patients expressed satisfaction with the nursing care they received. However, researchers widely recognise the difficulties involved in measuring patient satisfaction and the tendency to obtain positive evaluations of care when patients are still hospitalised. But only 12% expressed general satisfaction with their hospital stay. On balance, the effect of the shift on patient views appears to be neutral, although strongly negative views were expressed in general terms about the length of the nurses' day under a 12-hour shift and nurses' fatigue. Disquiet was also expressed about the possible risk to which they, as consumers, might be exposed as a result of the long day *(15)*.

Nurses' attitudes

The survey of some 1800 nurses working the 12-hour shift in the various hospitals run by the health board revealed an interesting pattern in the attitudes of nurses towards continuing to work the shift *(15, 16, 18, 22)*. The findings suggest that the older the nurse, the more likely she is to be married, live further from hospital, have children and express negative attitudes toward the 12-hour shift because of the disruption it can have on family life *(15,22)*. It is interesting to note that reported fatigue levels at the end of the day were not associated with nurses' age thus discounting a simple age effect hypothesis. The 12-hour shift may also have a negative effect on recruitment; some 65.57% of respondents indicated they felt it would make returning to nursing a less attractive prospect *(15,22)*.

When asked if they were in favour of continuing to work 12-hour shifts, a third of all nurses indicated they were in favour, half against and the rest unsure *(Table 1)*. There were general differences between hospitals with the 12-hour shift being generally liked in some but disliked in others. These differences are perhaps most interestingly revealed by considering nurses' reported feelings about the shift in relation to the sort of ward in which they work *(Table 1)*.

Although somewhat polarised, the psychiatric and mental handicap nurses were, as a group, more in favour of the 12-hour shift than general nurses *(Table 1)*. Clearly this is an important finding, but it is not easy to explain. For example, it may reflect differences in the nature of the work involved. Or it may relate to how long the 12-hour shift had been in operation at the various hospitals; the shift had been worked longest in some psychiatric wards. Finally, this finding may well reflect the preference of the higher proportion of males who work in psychiatric and mental handicap nursing, or a complex interaction of all of these factors.

Our questionnaire also contained a job satisfaction scale (26) for two factors: intrinsic satisfaction (the vocational aspect of nursing) and extrinsic satisfaction (pay). Overall, under the 12-hour shift, the nurses were significantly less intrinsically and extrinsically satisfied than under the eight-hour shift (16).

Type of unit	In favour/ strongly in favour	Against/ strongly against	Undecided or no preference
	%	%	%
Psychiatric & mental handicap	40.9	36.9	22.2
Acute medical	40.9	45.7	13.4
Acute surgical	30.1	50.0	19.9
Geriatric	26.3	58.3	15.4
Specialised*	21.2	64.7	14.1
Crisis†	20.3	59.4	20.3
Maternity & neonatal	13.2	76.9	9.9
All general nurses	26.1	58.5	15.3
Psychiatric & mental handicap	40.9	36.9	22.2
All nurses# (n = 1 038)	33.1	49.6	17.3

* eg.ENT; Dermatology; Paediatrics
†eg. Theatre; A&E; ITUs
#The number of nurses from whom there were valid responses to both the attitude and speciality questions.

Table 1 Nurses' reported feelings by speciality, about continuing to work the 12-hour shift

Fatigue levels

In order to look at fatigue levels we administered a memory and search task (MAST) to 51 volunteers over two complete days on duty. The MAST cognitive performance measure has been shown to be sensitive to time of day effect (27, 28) and was administered every two hours throughout the day. Half the subjects worked 12-hour shifts and half worked in comparable wards/specialities in hospitals working traditional shift systems. Thus we were able to investigate differences between eight and 12-hour shifts on cognition.

There were no obvious differences between the two shift systems in the patterning of performance on the tasks. Nurses' performance appeared to be in line with circadian rhythms rather than a simple function of the shift they were working (paper in preparation. Todd, C., Robinson, G., Reid, N.). These subjects also completed subjective visual analogue scales of their alertness and well-being. Here there were differences: those work-

ing the 12-hour shift reported becoming progressively more tired from a midday peak. However, the subjective rating did not correlate well with the MAST scores.

The interpretation here needs some care. The subjects were competing heavily under both shift systems to perform as well as possible in front of their peers. Thus the MAST scores reflect those of highly motivated, practised subjects. On the other hand, it seems possible that, given the negative attitudes towards the 12-hour shift system, the subjective ratings formed part of the group's rhetoric of complaint against the shift system (18, 29, 30, 31).

Summary and conclusions

In comparison to the more traditional eight-hour shift, our results show that a 12-hour shift had the following effects:

1. There was a lower quality of patient care overall, which appeared to affect most adversely the most dependent patients.
2. There was less direct patient care throughout the day and this was especially marked during the later period of the day.
3. Nurse education appeared to have suffered, in that trained nurses supervised students less and when they were paired up there was less observed educational activity.
4. There was little effect on patient satisfaction but patients expressed some disquiet as to risk to themselves.
5. The 12-hour shift was not universally accepted nor liked by nurses. When it was liked, this appears to be related to lifestyle.
6. There were, however, no differences between nurses working eight and 12-hour shifts in terms of cognitive performance through the day.

Clearly, attitudes and behaviours are interrelated and it is difficult to unravel the causal relationships which may exist between shift preferences and behaviour. Moreover, we did not detect any advantage to 12-hour shifts in terms of staffing levels during the day and our behavioural data would suggest that no advantage accrued from the reduction in overlaps. While we must stress that we found no evidence that the 12-hour shift put individual patients at greater risk, the balance of the evidence we collected must militate against introducing 12-hour shifts.

If a ward or unit decides to try 12-hour shifts it should be done with careful monitoring of the effects of the change. Hospital and ward managers, as well as staff, must be ready to take remedial steps if necessary.

On the basis of this research evidence and the difficulties which would be involved in running such evaluation programmes, there would seem to be little justification in introducing 12-hour shifts.

References

1 Underwood, A.B. What a twelve-hour shift offers. *American Journal of Nursing* 1975; 75: 7, 1176-1178
2 Ganong, W. L., Ganong, J. M., Harrison, E. T. The twelve-hour shift: better quality, lower cost. *Journal of Nursing Administration* 1976; 6: 2, 17-29
3 McColl, C. M. Twelve-hour shifts, a way to beat the 'prime-time' blues. *The Canadian Nurse* 1982; 78: 11, 28-31
4 Metcalf, M.L. The twelve-hour weekend plan - does the nursing staff really like it? *Journal of Nursing Administration* 1982; 12:19, 16-19
5 McGillick, K. Modifying schedules makes jobs more satisfying. *Nursing Management* 1983; 14:1, 53-55
6 Stinson, S.M., Hazlett, C.B. Nurse and physician opinion of a modified work week trial. *Journal of Nursing Administration* 1975; 5: pt 7, 21026
7 Vik. A.G., MacKay, R.C. How does the twelve-hour shift affect patient care? *Journal of Nursing Administration* 1982 12: pt 11, 11-14
8 Blanchflower, S. Alternative rota systems. *Nursing Times* 1986; 12: 4, 55-58
9 Johnston, M., Pollard, B., Manktelow, a. Length of nursing shift: stress and information processing. *The Psychologist* 1989; 2: (supp) 78
10 Libre, E. The good and the bad of twelve-hour shifts. *Registered Nurse* 1975; 38: 47-52
11 Hibberd, J.M. 12-hour shifts for nursing staff: A field experiment. *Hospital Administration in Canada* 1973; 15:26-30
12 Bajnok, I. The twelve-hour shift: 'It's good for nurses, but is it good for patients?' *Hospital Administration in Canada* 1975; 17: 25-36
13 Eaton, P., Gottselig, S. Effects of longer hours, shorter weeks for intensive care nurses. *Dimensions in Health Services* 1980; 57: 8, 25-27
14 Crump, K., Newson, P. Implementing the twelve-hour shift: a case history. *Hospital Administration in Canada* 1975; 17: 20-24
15 Reid, N., Robinson, G., Todd, C. *Evaluation of the Twelve-Hour Shift System in Nursing.* Coleraine: University of Ulster, Centre for Applied Health Studies, 1988
16 Todd, C., Reid, N., Robinson, G. Twelve versus eight-hour shifts: Job satisfaction of nurses and quality of care provided. *The Psychologist* 1989; 2: (supp), 98
17 Todd, C., Reid, N., Robinson G. The quality of nursing care under eight-hour and twelve-hour shifts: A repeated measures study. *International Journal of Nursing Studies* 1989; 26: 4, 359-368
18 Todd, C. Changes in temporal structuring and health care delivery. *The Psychologist* 1990; 3: (supp), 27
19 Reid, N., Robinson, G., Todd, C. The quantity of nursing care on wards working eight-hour and twelve-hour shifts. *International Journal of Nursing Studies* 1991; 28: 1, 47-54
20 Reid, N., Todd, C., Robinson, G. Educational activities on wards under twelve hour shifts. *International Journal of Nursing Studies* (in press)
21 Reid, N., Todd, C., Robinson, G. The twelve-hour shift and its impact on nursing education: the views of nurse educators and students. *International Journal of Nursing Studies* (in press)
22 Todd, C., Robinson, G., Reid, N. Nurses' attitudes towards twelve hour shifts. *International Journal of Nursing Studies* (in press)
23 Goldstone, L.A., Ball, J.A., Collier, M.M. MONITOR: *An index of the quality of nursing care for acute medical and surgical wards.* Newcastle-upon-Tyne: Newcastle-upon-Tyne Polytechnic Products, 1983
24 Illsely, V.A., Goldstone, L.A. *A guide to MONITOR for Nursing Staff.* Newcastle-upon-Tyne: Newcastle-upon-Tyne Polytechnic Products, 1985
25 Jackson, M., McKague, L. *How to implement the HSSG patient Classification – A manual.* Saskatchewan: Hospital systems study Group, 1970
26 Clark, J. *Time Out? A study of absenteeism among nurses.* London: Royal College of Nursing, 1975
27 Folkard, S., Knauth, P., Monk, T.H. The effect of memory load on the circadian variation in performance efficiency under a rapidly rotating shift system. *Ergonomics* 1976; 19: 4, 479-488
28 Folkard, S., Monk, T.H., Lobban, M.C. Short and long-term adjustment of circadian rhythms in 'permanent' night nurses. *Ergonomics* 1978; 21: 785-799
29 Turner, B. *Medical Power and Social Knowledge* London: Sage, 1988: 146-156
30 Salaman, G. *Working.* London:

Tavistock, 1986

31 Michael, M. Intergroup theory and deconstruction. In: Parker, I., Shotter, J. (eds) *Deconstructing Social Psychology*. London: Routledge, 1990

This work was funded by a Northern Ireland Health Board Commission.
Chris Todd, Norma Reid and Gillian Robinson wrote this paper while at the Centre for Health and Social Research, University of Ulster, Northern Ireland. Chris Todd is now senior research associate, Dept. of Community Medicine, Cambridge University; Professor Reid is head of the Department of Health Services, Coventry Polytechnic and Ms Robinson is research officer at the Northern Ireland Regional Research Laboratory, Queen's University, Belfast, and the University of Ulster.

To believe or not to believe

RESOURCE 3

Griffiths, P. (1993), Nursing Times, 89 (1), January 6, p.39.

As King Lear said, 'How sharper than a serpent's tooth it is to have a thankless child', or did he? At any rate, I'm pretty sure that it was said by one of Shakespeare's characters. And my uncertainty serves to illustrate my point pretty well.

I had planned to begin by writing, 'To paraphrase Shakespeare, how sharper than a serpent's tooth it is to hear a nurse say "research has shown" ...' Then I realised I did not really know precisely what Shakespeare had written, or what exactly he had meant by it. Indeed, I began to doubt whether I knew who had written those words in the first place.

I could probably have found out the exact details, but my point is that often, when nursing colleagues utter the immortal phrase 'research has shown' they are doing what I have just done.

I would like to provide a few examples of the problems of quoting research.

First, if we assume that the person quoting the research is not deliberately lying, the findings themselves may still not be all they appear to be.

For example, Sir Cyril Burt published many studies purporting to show that academic ability was largely inherited. For decades his work was quoted extensively in most standard education and psychology textbooks.

The trouble is that he made up a lot of his so-called research. The fraud was discovered only after his death, when a researcher looked for his original data and realised that they were not based on any research at all.

While academic fraud on the scale of Sir Cyril's is rare, it proves my point - don't believe all you read. Many researchers will make claims for their work which overstate its significance. Only by going to the original research reports can you avoid falling for someone's subjective interpretation of the work.

Second, it is important to remember that statistics in themselves cannot tell you anything, so they cannot themselves lie. They can, however, be tailored to tell you things they do not.

For example, most people with AIDS are found to have antibodies to the HIV virus. Statistics suggest that this is unlikely to be coincidence and that there is a strong correlation between HIV infection and AIDS. There is also a less strong correlation between having AIDS and of abusing drugs intravenously or being a homosexual male. Without further evidence it would be easy to misinterpret the statistics.

The most well-substantiated theory states that the HIV virus causes AIDS and the evidence to support this draws on statistics. But without a plausible theory to explain the cause of AIDS, the statistics would show nothing.

It is for this reason that the correlation between AIDS, HIV and intravenous drug abuse cannot be used to prove that having HIV causes drug abuse or homosexuality. For the same reason, the correlation does not, as some would have you believe, show that homosexuality causes AIDS.

The third point to look at is that something that is true for a particular case in particular circumstances may not be true in slightly altered circumstances.

It is often stated, for example, that research has shown that giving patients information preoperatively on levels of pain after surgery helps to reduce anxiety and so lessens postoperative pain. However, I could state that I suspect (although I have nothing to back this up) that information given by some consultants I have met would do nothing to reduce the average patient's anxiety levels.

Complex situations can rarely be fully explained by simple statements derived from single research studies.

Now for my fourth point. On one occasion I was told that 'research had shown' that acupressure was an effective method of controlling chemotherapy-induced nausea. I was given a reference to an article which stated that some of the author's patients had found acupressure beneficial. However, I was also referred to several similar articles quoting the first, plus a study whose methodology was, to put it charitably, open to question.

Just because it is written down does not mean it is research. Just because the author quotes Bloggs (1992) as 'showing' something, does not mean that Bloggs did any original research.

We must learn to use research properly. If somebody quotes findings which will affect your practice, do not simply accept them because the person who said it appears to know what he or she is talking about, or because it accords with what you think. If there is an established body of research, a good starting point is to turn to standard texts for summaries of various authors' works. There is no substitute for getting as near as possible to the original research.

Research-based practice will be liberating when it happens; reading and researching an area is challenging and exciting. Simply doing something on the say-so of someone who tells you that 'research has shown' will lead to unquestioning, possibly dangerous, ritualised practice. Does that sound familiar?

Peter Griffiths, BA, RGN, is clinical researcher, Camberwell Nursing Development Unit, King's College Hospital, London.

RESOURCE 4

Polit, D. and Hungler, B. (1989) in Essentials of Nursing Research, Philadelphia: Lippincott, pp. 348-360

The Report
The role of health-care providers in teenage pregnancy
by Phyllis Nelson 1987

Background

Of the 20 million teenagers living in the United States today, approximately one in five is sexually active by age 14; 50% have had sexual intercourse by age 19 (Kelman and Saner, 1979). Despite increased availability of contraceptives to teenagers, the number of teenage pregnancies has risen at an alarming rate over the past few years. Over one million girls under age 20 become pregnant each year and, of these, about 500,000 become teenage mothers (U.S. Bureau of the Census, 1980). Dr. Robert Toll, director of the Obstetrics Department of an inner-city Detroit hospital, has commented, 'Pregnancy among adolescents is one of the most stubborn problems facing obstetrical staff today' (Toll, 1978, p.5).

Public concern regarding the teenage pregnancy epidemic stems not only from the rising number of involved teenagers, but also from the extensive research that has documented the adverse consequences of early parenthood in the health arena. Pregnant teenagers have been found to receive less prenatal care (Tremain, 1975), to be more likely to develop toxemia (Schendley, 1976; Waters, 1973), to be more likely to experience prolonged labor (Curran, 1979), to be more likely to have low birth weight babies (Tremain, 1975; Beach, 1980), and to have babies with lower Apgar scores (Beach, 1980) than older mothers. The long-term conse-quences to the teenage mothers themselves are also extremely bleak: teenage mothers get less schooling, are more likely to be on public assistance, are likely to earn lower wages, and are more likely to get divorced if they marry than their peers who postpone parenthood (Jamail, 1981; Weissbach, 1976; North, 1978; Smithfield, 1979).

The one million teenagers who become pregnant each year are caught up in a tough emotional decision - to carry the pregnancy to term and keep the baby, to have an abortion, or to deliver the baby and surrender it for adoption. Despite the widely reported adverse consequences of young parenthood cited above, most young women today are opting for delivery and child rearing (Jaffrey, 1978; Henderson, 1977).

The purpose of this study was to test the effectiveness of a special intervention based in an out-patient clinic of a Chicago hospital in improving the health outcomes of a group of pregnant teenagers. Specifically, it was hypothesized that pregnant teenagers who were in the special program would receive more prenatal care, would be less likely to develop toxemia, would be less likely to have a low birth weight baby, would spend fewer hours in labor, would have babies with higher Apgar scores, and would be more likely to use a contraceptive at 6 months postpartum than pregnant teenagers not enrolled in the program.

The theoretical model on which this research was based is an ecological model of personal behavior (Brandenburg, 1979). A schematic diagram of the ecological model is presented in *Figure 13-1*. In this framework, the actions of the person are the focus of attention, but those actions are believed to be a function not only of the person's own characteristics, attitudes, and abilities but also a function of other influences in their environment. Environmental influences can be differentiated according to their proximal relationship with the target person. Health-care workers and institutions are, according to the model, more distant influences than the family, peers, and boyfriends. Yet it is assumed that these less immediate forces are real and can intervene to change the behaviors of the target person. Thus, it is hypothesized that pregnant teenagers can be influenced by increased exposure to a health-care team providing a structured program of services designed to promote improved health outcome.

Methods

A special program of services for pregnant teenagers was implemented in the out-patient clinic of an inner-city public hospital in Chicago. The intervention involved nutrition education and counselling, parenting education, instruction on prenatal health care, preparation for childbirth, and contraceptive counselling.

All teenagers with a confirmed pregnancy attending the clinic were asked if they wanted to participate in the special program. The goal was to enroll 150 pregnant teenagers during the program's first year of operation. A total of 276 teenagers attending the clinic were invited to participate; of these, 59 had an abortion or miscarriage and 108 declined to participate, yielding an experimental group sample of 109 girls.

To test the effectiveness of the special program, a comparison group of pregnant teenagers was needed. Another inner-city hospital agreed to cooperate in the study. Staff obtained information on the labor and delivery outcomes of the 120 teenagers who delivered at the comparison hospital, where no special teen-parent program was available. For both experimental group and comparison group subjects, a follow-up telephone interview was conducted six months postpartum to determine if the teenagers were using birth control.

The independent variable in this study was the teenager's program status: experimental group members participated in the special program while comparison group members did not. The dependent variables were the teenagers' labor-delivery and postpartum contraceptive outcomes. The operational definitions of the dependent variables were as follows:

Prenatal care: Number of visits made to a physician/nurse during the pregnancy, exclusive of the visit for the pregnancy test;

Toxemia: Presence versus absence of preeclamptic toxemia as diagnosed by a physician;

Labor time: Number of hours elapsed from the first contractions until delivery of the baby, to the nearest half hour;

Low infant birth weight: Birth weights of less than 2,500 grams versus those of 2,500 grams or greater;

Apgar score: Infant Apgar score (from 0 to 10) taken at three minutes after birth;

Contraceptive use postpartum: Self-reported use of any form of birth control six months postpartum versus self-reported nonuse.

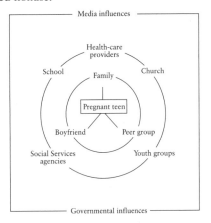

Figure 13-1 Model of ecological contexts

The two groups were compared on these six outcome measures using t-test and chi-squared tests.

Results

The teenagers in the sample were, on average, 17.6 years old at the time of delivery. The mean age was 17.1 in the experimental group and 18.0 in the comparison group.

By definition, all the teenagers in the experimental group had received prenatal care. Two of the teenagers in the comparison group had no health-care treatment prior to delivery. The distribution of visits for the two groups is presented in *Figure 13-2*. The experimental group had a higher mean number of prenatal visits than the comparison group, as shown in *Table 13-1*, but the difference was not statistically significant at the .05 level, using a t-test for independent groups.

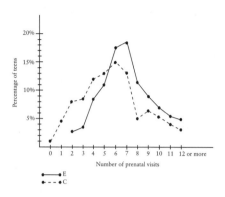

Figure 13-2 Frequency distribution of prenatal visits, by experimental versus comparison group. (E = experimental group; C = comparison group)

In the sample as a whole, about one girl in ten was diagnosed as having preeclamptic toxemia. The difference between the two groups was in the hypothesized direction with 1.6% more of the comparison group teenagers developing this complication. However, the group difference in percentages was not significant using a chi-squared test.

The hours spent in labor ranged from 3.5 to 29.0 in the experimental group and from 4.5 to 33.5 in the comparison group. On average, teenagers in the experimental group spent 14.3 hours in labor, compared with 15.2 for the comparison group teenagers. The difference was not statistically significant.

With regard to low birth weight babies, a total of 43 girls out of 229 in the sample gave birth to babies who weighed under 2,500 grams (5.5 pounds). More of the comparison group teenagers (20.9%) than experimental group teenagers (16.5%) had low birth weight babies but, once again, the difference was not significant.

The three-minute Apgar score in the two groups was quite similar: 7.3 for the experimental group and 6.7 for the comparison group. This small difference was not significant.

Finally, the teenagers were compared with respect to their adoption of birth control six months after delivering their babies. For this variable, teenagers were coded as users of contraception if they were either using some method of birth control at the time of the follow-up interview or if they were nonusers but were sexually inactive (i.e were using abstinence to prevent a repeat pregnancy). The results of the chi-squared test revealed that a significantly higher percentage of experimental group teenagers (81.7%) than comparison group teenagers (62.5%) were using birth control after delivery. This difference was significant beyond the .01 level.

Discussion

The results of this evaluation were disappointing, but not discouraging. There was only one outcome for which a significant difference was observed. The experimental program significantly increased the percentage of teenagers who used birth control after delivering their babies. Thus, one highly important result of participating in the program is that an early repeat pregnancy will be postponed. There is abundant research that has shown that repeat pregnancy among teenagers is especially damaging to their educational and occupational attainment and leads to particularly adverse labor and delivery outcomes in the higher-order births (Klugman, 1975; Jackson, 1978).

The experimental group had more prenatal care, but not significantly more. Perhaps part of the difficulty is that the program can only begin to deliver services once pregnancy has been diagnosed. If a teenager does not come in for a pregnancy test until her fourth or fifth month, this obviously puts an upper limit on the number of visits she will have; it also gives less

Outcome Variable	Group Experimental (N=109)	Comparison (N=120)	Difference	Test Statistic
Mean number of prenatal visits	7.1	5.9	1.2	$t=1.83, df=227$,NS
Percentage with toxemia	10.1%	11.7%	−1.6%	$X^2=0.15, df=1$,NS
Mean hours spent in labor	14.3	15.2	−0.9	$t=1.01, df=227$,NS
Percentage with low birth weight baby	16.5	20.9	−4.4%	$X^2=0.71, df=1$,NS
Mean Apgar score	7.3	6.7	0.6	$t=0.98, df=227$,NS
Percentage adopting contraception postpartum	81.7%	62.5%	19.2	$X^2=10.22, df=1,$ $p<.01$

Table 13-1 Summary of experimental / comparison group differences

time for her to eat properly, avoid smoking and drinking, and take other steps to enhance her health during pregnancy. Thus, one implication of this finding is that the program needs to do more to encourage early pregnancy screening. Perhaps a joint effort between the clinic personnel and school nurses in neighboring middle schools and high schools could be launched to publicize the need for a timely pregnancy test and to inform teenagers where such a test could be obtained.

The two groups performed similarly with respect to the various labor and delivery outcomes chosen to evaluate the effectiveness of the new program. The issue of timeliness is again relevant here. The program may have been delivering services too late in the pregnancy for the instruction to have made much of an impact on the health of the mother and her child. This interpretation is supported, in part, by the fact that the one variable for which timeliness was not an issue (postpartum contraception) was, indeed, positively affected by program participation. Another possible implication is that the program itself should be made more powerful, for example, by lengthening or adding to instruction sessions.

Given that the experimental-comparison differences were all in the hypothesized direction, it is also tempting to criticize the sample size. A larger sample (which was originally planned) might have yielded some significant differences.

In summary, the experimental intervention is not without promise. A particularly exciting finding is that participation in the program resulted in better contraceptive use, which will presumably lower the incidence of repeat pregnancy. It would be interesting to follow these teenagers two years after delivery to see if the groups differ in the rates of repeat pregnancy. It appears that more needs to be done to get these teenagers into the program early in their pregnancies. Perhaps then the true effectiveness of the program would be demonstrated.

Critique of the research report

In the following discussion we present some comments regarding the quality of various aspects of this fictitious research report. Students are urged to read the report and formulate their own opinions about its strengths and weaknesses prior to reading this critique. An evaluation of a study is necessarily partly subjective. Therefore, it should be expected that students might disagree with some of the points made below. Other students will also criticize some aspects of the study that we do not comment on. However, we believe that most of the serious methodological flaws of the study are highlighted in our critique.

Title

The title for the study is misleading. The research does not investigate the role of health-care professionals in serving the needs of pregnant teenagers. A more appropriate title would be 'Health-Related Outcomes of an Intervention for Pregnant Teenagers'.

Background

The background section of this report consists of three distinct elements that can be analyzed separately: a literature review, statement of the problem, and a theoretical framework.

The literature is relatively clearly written and well-organized. It serves the important function of establishing a need for the experimental program by documenting how widespread the problem of teenage pregnancy is and what some of the adverse consequences of teenage pregnancy are.

However, the literature review could be improved. First, an inspection of the citations suggests that the author is not as up-to-date on research relating to teenage pregnancy as she might have been. Most of the references are from the 1970s, often the mid-70s, meaning that this literature is over a decade old. Second, there is material in the literature review section that is not relevant and should be removed. For example, the paragraph on the options with which a pregnant teenager is faced are among the most critical extraneous variables: subjects' social class/family income, age, race/ethnicity, parity, participation in another pregnant teenager program, marital status, and prepregnancy experience with contraception (for the postpartum contraception outcome). The researcher should have attempted to gather information on these variables from experimental group and comparison group teenagers and from eligible teenagers in the experimental hospital who declined to participate in the program. To the extent that these three groups are similar on these variables, the credibility of the internal validity of the study would be enhanced. If sizable differences are observed, the researcher would at least know or suspect the direction of the biases and could factor that information into her interpretation and conclusions.

Had the researcher gathered information on the extraneous variables, another possibility would have been to match experimental and comparison group subject on one or two variables, such as social class and age. Matching is not an ideal method of controlling extraneous variables; for one thing, matching on two variables would not equate the two groups in terms of the other extraneous variables. However, matching is preferable to doing nothing.

So far, we have focused our attention on the research design, but other aspects of the study are also problematic. Let us consider the decision the researcher made about the population. The target population is not explicitly defined by the researcher, but one can infer that the target population is pregnant girls under age 20 who carry their infants to delivery. The accessible population is pregnant teenagers from one area in Chicago. Is it reasonable to assume that the accessible population is representative of the target population? No, it is not. It is likely that the accessible population is quite different from the overall population in terms of family income, race/ethnicity, access to health care, family intactness, and many other characteristics. The researcher should have more clearly discussed exactly who the target population of the research was.

Nelson would have done well, in fact, to delimit the target population; had she done so, it might have been possible to control some of the extraneous variables discussed previously. For example, Nelson could have established eligibility criteria that excluded multigravidas, very young teenagers (e.g under age 15), or married teenagers. Such a specification would have limited the generalizability of the findings, but it would have enhanced the internal validity of the study because it probably would have increased the comparability of the experimental and comparison groups.

The sample was a sample of convenience, the least effective sampling design. There is no way of knowing whether the sample represents the accessible and target populations. While probability sampling was probably not feasible, the researcher might have improved her sampling design by using a quota sampling plan. For example, if the researcher knew that in the accessible population, 50% of the families received public assistance, then it might have been possible to enhance the representativeness of the samples by using a quota system to ensure that 50% of the research subjects came from welfare-dependent families.

Sample size is a difficult issue. Many of the reported results were in the hypothesized direction but were not significant.

When this is the case, the adequacy of the sample size is always suspect, as Nelson pointed out. Each group had about 100 subjects. In many cases this sample size would be considered adequate, but in the present case it is not. One of the difficulties in testing the effectiveness of new interventions is that, generally, the experimental group is not being compared with a no-treatment group. Although the comparison group in this example was not getting the special program services, it cannot be assumed that this group was getting no services at all. Some comparison group members may have had ample prenatal care during which the health-care staff may have provided much of the same information as that taught in the special program. The point is not that the new program was not needed, but rather that unless an intervention is extremely powerful and innovative, the incremental improvement will typically be rather small. Whenever relatively small effects are anticipated, the sample must be very large in order for differences to be statistically significant. Although it is beyond the scope of this book to explain the power analysis calculations, it can be shown that in order to detect a significant difference between the two groups with respect, say, to the incidence of toxemia, a sample of over 5,000 pregnant teenagers would have been needed. Had the researcher done a power analysis prior to conducting the study, she might have realized the insufficiency of her sample for certain of the outcomes and might have developed a different sampling plan, and/or identified different dependent variables.

The fourth major methodological decision concerns the measurement of the research variables. For the most part, the researcher did a good job in selecting objective, reliable, and valid outcome measures. Also, her operational definitions were clearly worded and unambiguous. Two comments are in order, however. First, it might have been better to operationalize two of the variables differently. Infant birth weight might have been more sensitively measured as actual weight (a ratio-level measurement) or as a three-level ordinal variable ($<1,500$ grams; $>1,500$ but $<2,500$ grams; and $>2,500$ grams) instead of as a dichotomous variable. The contraceptive variable could also have been operationalized to yield a more sensitive (i.e. more discriminating) measure. Rather than measuring contraceptive use as a dichotomy, Nelson could have created an ordinal scale based on either frequency of use (eg. 0%, 1-25%, 26-50%, 51-75%, and 76-100% of the time) or on the effectiveness of the type of birth control used.

A second consideration is whether the outcome variables adequately captured the effects of program activities. It might have been easier, with the small sample of 229 teens, and more directly relevant to capture group differences in, say, dietary practices during pregnancy than in infant birth weight. None of the outcome variables measured the effects of parenting education. In other words, the researcher could have added more direct measures of the effect of the special program.

One other point about the methods should be made, and that relates to ethical considerations. The article does not specifically say that subjects were asked for their informed consent, but that does not necessarily mean that no written consent was obtained. It is quite likely that the experimental group subjects, when asked to volunteer for the special program, were advised about their participation in the study, and asked to sign a consent form. But what about the control group subjects? The article implies that comparison group members were given no opportunity to decline participation and were not aware of having their birth outcomes used as data in the research. In some cases, this procedure is acceptable. For example, a hospital or clinic might agree to release patient information without the patients' consent if the release of such information is done anonymously - that is, if it can be provided in such a way that even the researcher does not know the identity of the patients. In the present study, however, it is clear that the names of the comparison subjects were given to the researcher, since she had to contact the comparison group at six months postpartum to determine their contraceptive practices. Thus, this study does not appear to have adequately safeguarded the rights of the comparison group subjects.

In summary, the researcher appears not to have adhered to ethical procedures, and she also failed to really give the new program a fair test. Nelson should have taken a number of steps to control extraneous variables and should have attempted to get a larger sample (even if this meant waiting for additional subjects to enroll in the program). In addition to concerns about the internal validity of the study, its generalizability is also questionable.

Results

Nelson did a good job of presenting the results of the study. The presentation was straightforward and succinct and was enhanced by the inclusion of a good table and figures. The style of this section was also appropriate: it was written objectively and was well-organized.

The statistical analyses were also reasonably well done. The descriptive statistics (means and percentages) were appropriate for the level of measurement of the variables. The author did not, however, provide any information about the variability of the measures, except for noting the range for the "time spent in labor" variable. *Figure 13-2* suggests that the two groups did differ in variability: the comparison group was more heterogeneous than the experimental group with regard to prenatal care received.

The two types of inferential statistics used (the t-test and chi-squared test) were also appropriate, given the levels of measurement of the outcome variables. The results of these tests were efficiently presented in a single table. It should be noted that there are more powerful statistics available that could have been used to control extraneous variables (e.g. analysis of covariance), but in the present study, it appears that the only extraneous variable that could have been controlled through statistical procedures was the subjects' age, because no data were apparently collected on other extraneous variables (social class, ethnicity, parity, and so on).

Discussion

Nelson's discussion section fails almost entirely to take the study's limitations into account in interpreting the data. The one exception is her acknowledgment that the sample size was too small. She seems unconcerned about the many threats to the internal or external validity of her research.

Nelson lays almost all the blame for the nonsignificant findings on the program rather than on the research methods. She feels that two aspects of the program should be changed: (1) recruitment of teenagers into the program earlier in their pregnancies and (2) strengthening program services. Both recommendations might be worth pursuing, but there is little in the data themselves to suggest these modifications.

With nonsignificant results such as those that predominated in this study, there are two possibilities to consider: (1) the results are accurate; the program is not effective for those outcomes examined (though it might be effective for other measures) and (2) the results are false; the existing program is effective for the outcomes examined, but the tests failed to demonstrate it. Nelson concluded that the first possibility was correct and therefore recommended that the program be changed. Equally plausible is the possibility that the study methods were too weak to demonstrate the program's true effects.

We do not have enough information about the characteristics of the sample to conclude with certainty that there were substantial selection biases. We do, however, have a clue that selection biases were operative in a direction that would make the program look less effective than it actually is. Nelson noted in the beginning of the results section that the average age of the teenagers in the experimental group was 17.1, compared with 18.0 in the comparison group. Age is inversely related to positive labor and delivery outcomes: indeed, that is the basis for having a special program for teenage mothers. Therefore, the experimental group's performance on the outcome measures was possibly depressed by the youth of that group. Had the two groups been equivalent in terms of age, the group differences might have been larger and could have reached levels of statistical significance. Other uncontrolled pretreatment differences could also have masked true treatment effect.

For the one significant outcome, we cannot rule out the possibility that a Type-I error was made - that is, that the null hypothesis was in fact true. Again, selection biases could have been operative. The experimental group might have contained many more girls who had preprogram experience with contraception; it might have contained more highly motivated teenagers, or more single teenagers, or more teenagers who had already had multiple pregnancies than the comparison group. There is simply no way of knowing whether the significant outcome reflects true program effectiveness or merely initial group differences.

Aside from Nelson's disregard for the problems of internal validity, the author definitely overstepped the bounds of scholarly speculation by reading too much into her data. She unquestionably assumed that the program caused contraceptive improvements: 'the experimental program significantly increased the percentage of teenagers who used birth control ...'. Worse yet, she went on to conclude that repeat pregnancies will be postponed in the experimental group, although she does not know whether the teenagers used an effective contraception, whether they used it all the time, or whether they used it correctly.

As another example of 'going beyond the data,' Nelson became overly invested in her notion that teenagers need greater and earlier exposure to the program. It is not that her hypothesis has no merit - the problem is that she builds an elaborate rationale for program changes with no apparent empirical support. She probably had information on when in the pregnancy the teenagers entered the program, but that information was not shared with readers. Her argument about the need for more publicity on early screening would have had more clout if she had reported that the majority of teenagers entered the program during the fourth month of their pregnancies or later. Additionally, she could have marshalled more evidence in support of her proposal if she had been able to show that earlier entry into the program was associated with better health outcomes. For example, she could have compared the outcomes of teenagers entering the program in the first, second, and third trimesters of their pregnancies.

In conclusion, the study is not without some merit. As Nelson noted, there is some reason to be cautiously optimistic that the program could have some beneficial effects. However, the existing study is too seriously flawed to reach any conclusions, even tentatively. A replication with improved research methods is clearly needed to solve the research problem.

RESOURCE 5

Brown, J., Meikkle, J. and Webb, C. (1991), Nursing Times, 87 (13), March 27, pp. 49-52.

Collecting midstream specimens of urine – The research base

The study reported here, which is based on an undergraduate dissertation, analyses the content of medical and nursing articles published between 1956 and 1989 which consider the collection of mid stream specimens of urine (MSSUs). Subjective or qualitative and objective or quantitative content analyses were performed. A large disparity was discovered between the results of the two methods of analysis, implying that this research base cannot be translated into recommendations for collecting MSSUs.

It is often the simplest procedures that are most in need of scrutiny, for these are the aspects of nursing practice which are taken for granted and have become firmly incorporated into the routine fabric of nursing (1).

The collection of MSSUs is just such a task and one which does not inspire interest or enthusiasm among researchers. Smith (2) describes it as one of the least glamorous aspects of nursing, while Mellings (3) refers to the procedure as a nightmare.

Nonetheless, nurses are required to collect thousands of urine specimens every day for a variety of reasons. The majority are obtained in order to detect the presence of bacteria in the urine, while others are used to diagnose pregnancy or metabolic, hepatic, endocrine or other disorders (4). As the methods of collection vary widely, depending on the purpose of the investigation, only samples collected to detect bacteriuria are considered in this study.

MSSUs are collected routinely in both hospitals and the community. Stronge (5) calculates that approximately 39 samples are collected per hospital bed per year, while Werman (6) notes that between two and five per cent of all visits to general practitioners are associated with bacteriuria. It is clear, therefore, that this is an area of nursing practice sufficiently important to warrant further study.

Before the 1950s, urine specimens were obtained by urethral catheterisation to avoid contamination. However, this method was time-consuming, embarrassing for patients, and carried the risk of actually introducing bacteria into the urinary tract (7,8,9). Kass (10) concluded that 95% of all infections caused by Gram-negative bacteria could be diagnosed by counting bacterial culture counts, but the method was accurate only if the mid-portion of the sample was obtained after the external genitalia had been thoroughly cleaned and the sample was processed promptly in the laboratory. Failure to meet any of these criteria would affect both the sensitivity and specificity of the test.

Gram-positive bacteria are pathogenic in much smaller numbers (11) and there is thus an even smaller margin for error when differentiating between infection and contamination of specimens.

Kass's approach was embraced by the medical profession but as a result many patients, especially women, have been subjected to great indignities in the quest for the perfect urine sample. Women have been instructed to 'scrub' their genitalia with solutions as diverse as perchloride of mercury (12) and harsh antiseptics (13),

while Boshell and Sanford (14) felt it necessary for patients to sit in sitz baths filled with green soap for five minutes before they were deemed sufficiently clean to provide a urine sample. Women have also been encouraged to adopt diverse positions while micturating, including the lithotomy position (14), straddling wash-basins (12), standing (13), and sitting backwards on the toilet seat facing the lifted lid (14).

The collection of urine samples, then, is not as straightforward as it appears. Many variables affect the confidence which can be placed in the test results and it is the nurse, who is so often the person to obtain these specimens, who must be aware of the issues involved so that she can adopt a suitable collecting technique.

This study attempts to determine from the literature how specimens of urine should be collected from adult patients. Those who are very young, who do not speak English, who are menstruating, who are bedridden, who are mentally disturbed, or who are known to be suffering from congenital abnormalities of the genito-urinary tract are recognised as having special problems and cannot be discussed in a study of this size.

Content analysis

Content analysis is defined by Polit and Hungler (15) as the method for the objective, systematic and quantitative description of communications and documentary evidence. The purpose of content analysis, according to Abraham et al.(16) is to amalgamate the work of others in order to determine how the independent variables affect the dependent variables. In other words, it provides a synthesis or summary of all the research findings in a given area. The findings can then be used, for example by health-care professionals in deciding how to practise or, if the area of research is incomplete, they can provide a starting point for further study.

Qualitative content analysis

Qualitative content analysis consists of a study of the texts under consideration in order to identify themes which emerge. There may be a quantitative aspect, in that the number of occurrences of themes may be counted to give an impression of the relative importance of these themes in terms of the amount of attention they are given by writers. Interpretations of the text may then be made by the researcher on the basis of these findings. However, it is essential to bear in mind that the validity of the content analysis depends on the quality of the data on which it is based - in this case previously published research reports.

Variable	Women	Men
Portion of the sample	Mid and/or final	Mid and/or final
Cleansing agent	Soap	None
Rinsing agent	Water	Not applicable
Direction of cleansing	Anterior to posterior	Not applicable
Time interval	2 hours at room temperature or 48 hours if stored at 4°C or 72 hours if preserved in boric acid	2 hours at room temperature or 48 hours if stored at 4°C or 72 hours if preserved in boric acid
Person collecting	Patient	Patient
Method of instruction	Oral	Oral
Cleansing of hands	Yes	Yes
Retraction of genitalia	Yes	No
Time of collection	Early morning	Early morning

Table 1 Comparison of results of qualitative analyses in relation to women and men: categories which appear to lead to least contamination of specimens

The articles included in the present study were located using a MEDLINE search, a literature search performed by the Royal College of Nursing Library, the *Nursing Abstracts* (1970, 1989), and by following up articles which a previous author had considered to be important. These methods overlap to a certain extent, but their use gives a degree of confidence that all the relevant articles have been identified and included in the study, which is a fundamental pre-requisite of a valid content analysis *(17)*.

A review of the literature on the collection of MSSUs from 1956 to October 1989 indicates that there are 10 'themes' or independent variables associated with the collecting process. These are:

1 Portion of the urine sample.
2 Cleansing agent used to cleanse the urethral orifice.
3 Rinsing agent.
4 Direction of cleansing the perineum.
5 Time interval between collection of the sample and processing in the laboratory.
6 Person collecting the sample.
7 Method of instruction.
8 Cleansing of hands.
9 Retraction of the genitalia.
10 Time of collection of the sample.

These variables can also be divided into sub-divisions or smaller units which are called 'categories' *(18)*. For example, in this study the variable 'portion of the urine sample' has four categories, namely, any portion of the sample; initial portion of the sample; midstream portion of the sample; final portion of the sample.

The dependent variable is also categorical, for the sample can be sterile, contaminated or infected.

Qualitative content analysis of the articles reviewed suggests that the mid and/or final portion of the sample should be collected, with no cleansing for men but with soap cleansing from front to back and retracting the labia, followed by rinsing with water for women. Collection should be performed by the patient rather than a nurse, after receiving oral instructions and cleansing the hands. All specimens should be collected in the early morning, and may be stored for up to two hours at room temperatures or 48 hours at four degrees Centigrade. Alternatively, they may be preserved in boric acid prior to examination. These findings are summarised in *Table 1*.

Additional themes emerged from the review as extraneous variables which are possible influences on the results of MSSUs, and these were a diagnosis of diabetes mellitus; age, sex, and parity of the patient; whether the patient is or has recently been taking antibiotics, and whether a woman was pregnant at the time of collection of the sample.

Quantitative analysis

It became increasingly apparent during the literature review that it is very difficult to determine how urine samples should be collected by using qualitative analytic techniques. This is because the results of many of the studies were contradictory, and also because the large number of categories which had to be considered simultaneously made it impossible to determine which of the variables were relevant and which were not.

However, although the human brain cannot appreciate unaided the relative effect of each variable it does become possible to do this if statistical techniques are employed.

By using a statistical method known as logistic multiple regression analysis, relationships between the independent variables and the contamination and infection rates of the samples can be determined.

Following the advice of a statistician, the computer program GLIM Release 3.77 *(19)* was selected for the quantitative analysis. This program is specifically designed for logistic regression analysis where both the independent and dependent variables are categorical.

The main advantage of using this statistical approach is that it can 'weight' the results according to the size of the sample; that is, it will place more emphasis on the results from the larger studies than on those from smaller ones. It will also allow for 'unusual' results by modifying their weighting as necessary.

Data from several research reports had to be excluded from the analysis for various reasons. Two studies were omitted because their results were presented in the form of percentages rather than mean colonies of bacteria per millilitre, as in all the other studies. The statistical technique requires that all data are presented in the same format.

Other exclusions made from the sampling frame were those studies which involved male patients. This was done because it had become increasingly apparent during the qualitative analysis that the procedure required to obtain specimens from men was so different from that for women that it would be inappropriate to enter both sexes of patient into the same regression analysis.

Ideally, two separate analyses should be performed but only four studies were located which considered male subjects and there was, therefore, not sufficient data to allow this. Finally, 'cleansing of hands', 'time taken to deliver the specimen', 'antibiotic therapy' and 'diabetes' were rejected because inadequate data for comparison between studies was found in the articles reviewed. The exclusions resulted in a total of 51 categories which, following expert statistical advice, was considered acceptable because the sample was so large (a total of 33,956 urine specimens would be included in the analysis).

Variable	Qualitative analysis	Quantatitve analysis
Age	17-17 years and 70+ years	55 years
Pregnancy	Pregnant	Pregnant
Parity	Grand multigravida	Grand multigravida
Sexual activity	Sexually active	Not investigated
Diabetes mellitus	Diabetic	Not investigated
Antibiotic therapy	Not on therapy	Not investigated
Ethnic origin	Black patients	Black patients
Social class	Lower social class	Lower social class

Table 3 Comparison of results from both the qualitative and quantitative analyses for the extraneous variables which appear to increase the prevalence of bacteriuria within a population (female patients only)

Variable	Qualitative analysis	Quantative analysis
Portion of the sample	Mid and/or final	Any portion
Cleansing agent	Soap	Any agent
Rinsing agent	Water	Water
Direction of cleansing	Anterior to posterior	Not applicable
Time interval	2 hours at room temperature or 48 hours if stored at 4°C or 72 hours if preserved in boric acid	Not investigated
Person collecting	Patient	Health care professional
Method of instruction	Oral	Written
Cleansing of hands	Yes	Not investigated
Retraction of genitalia	Yes	Yes
Time of collection	Early morning	Not investigated

Table 2 Comparison of results from both qualitative and quantitative analyses for the variables in the collecting process: categories which appear to lead to least contamination of specimens (female patients only)

Analysing the results

Results of the analysis for the collecting process and for extraneous variables are shown in *Tables 1* and *2*, respectively.

Table 2 shows that the middle or final portion of the specimen was identified from the qualitative analyses as leading to lowest rates of infection being identified but, according to the quantitative analysis, any portion could be used.

With regard to cleansing agent, cleansing of the perineum appears to be a necessity rather than a ritual *(20)*. Soap was identified as the agent of choice from the qualitative analysis, whereas from *Table 1* it can be seen that there is very little difference in the effects of any of the disinfectants or soap, all of which lead to significantly lower infection rates.

However, if the results for cleansing agent are considered in juxtaposition with those for rinsing agent, it can be seen from *Table 1* that a rinsing agent such as water appears to increase the rate of contamination and infection identified.

This result suggests that if antiseptics are washed into the sample they will inhibit bacterial growth and lead to inaccurate categorisation of specimens, whereas rinsing with water removes this effect and gives higher, but more accurate, infection or contamination rates.

The increase in infection rate associated in *Table 2* with wiping away from the urethra is difficult to explain, and further research is needed. The significance level of the results is so great that it is unlikely to be a chance finding and, therefore, needs further investigation.

Time taken to process samples could not be investigated quantitatively because most researchers had ensured that the samples in their studies arrived and were processed in the laboratory within the recommended time limit.

There was disagreement between the two analyses also for 'person collecting the sample', qualitative analysis suggesting that this should be the patient but quantitative analysis suggesting that a health care professional should do this. A discrepancy for 'method of instruction' to patients was similarly identified.

The only area on which there was agreement in the two types of analysis was that patients should use their hands to retract their genitalia. However, not all studies compared retraction with non-retraction and so this finding again cannot be considered conclusive.

There was, however, substantially more affinity between the results from the two types of analysis in relation to the extraneous variables. Associations between the independent and dependent variables suggest that rates of bacteriuria are lower in patients who are male, below middle age, white, in higher socioeconomic groups, non-diabetic, or who are or have recently been taking antibiotics. The rate also seems to be lower for women who are not pregnant, not sexually active, and who have fewer than four children. These results are shown in *Table 3*.

Although the contradictory findings from the qualitative and quantitative analyses are disappointing in that they do not provide guidelines for practice, they have highlighted the need for further research.

Discussion

The most obvious question raised by this study is: could this review be used to define a standard method of collection of mid stream specimens of urine? The answer is unequivocally that it could not. The study, while comprehensive in that it includes a review of all the literature published in the area and is based on the results of 33,956 urine samples, is limited by the lack of internal validity in the studies included in the analysis.

Seaman and Verhonick *(21)* define internal validity as a measure of whether 'manipulation of the independent variable actually made a difference to the research findings'. It is clear that the researchers whose work is reviewed failed adequately to control all the variables associated with the process, making it very difficult accurately to determine relationships between the independent and dependent variables.

This problem of internal validity is one of the greatest drawbacks associated with content analysis.

Abraham *et al. (16)* note that, because the researcher has absolutely no control over what has been included in the previous studies, any limitations detected in the existing material will be unavoidably transferred into the current study.

However, it is important to realise that, although this study has not identified a sound research base which can be used to improve the standard of MSSU collection, it has succeeded in amalgamating the content of previously published material. As Polit and Hungler *(15)* note, research does not exist in a vacuum. In order for research findings to be useful, it is important that they should be an extension of previous knowledge as well as a guide for future activity.

It is hoped that this study has helped to indicate directions for future research by identifying possible associations between 19 variables and by defining for the first time differences between the extraneous variables and variables in the collecting process. It has also served to highlight areas where research is incomplete or inadequate, and it is, therefore, important to see the study as the beginning of the solution and not as the end.

In addition, having investigated the utility of logistic multiple regression analysis and the benefits of using both qualitative and quantitative methods of content analysis, a possible approach for a future study has been identified.

Subsequent researchers can ensure that only one variable is manipulated at a time and, by collecting relevant information about the characteristics of the subjects, will be able to collect a complete set of data which should allow less ambiguous results to be obtained.

In an article which traces the history of urine testing back to the time of the ancient Egyptians, Hatcher (22) notes that urinalysis has always involved a great deal more 'quackery and fraud' than 'scientific method'.

It has, of course, advanced from the days when diagnosis of disease was made purely on the basis of the colour and taste of the urine but, as this study has served to highlight, the practice is still more affected by traditions, myths and assumptions than it is by research evidence. It is to be hoped that nursing research will remedy this situation in the near future.

EDITOR'S COMMENTS

The more one studies something, the more one realises the difficulties and complexities. For a procedure viewed with such rigorous guidelines in procedure books, it could almost be predicted that the validity of these instructions should be questioned. Certainly this paper leads to more uncertainty and questioning. Nursing practitioners wishing desperately to base their care on research evidence cannot be blamed for feeling slightly frustrated, especially when research reports indicate one thing and authors' prescriptions something different.

Systematic reviews such as this one are rare and the use of meta-analysis is both testing and useful. Nursing literature is fraught with inconsistencies and this is not surprising when research studies on a relatively confined area raise so many contradictions. This clearly shows that it is only consistency and replication which can produce guidelines for nursing practice.

Anyone who has suffered a urinary infection would confirm that there cannot be many areas more important to the welfare of the patient. The agony associated with this in the first place is bad enough but the subsequent delay cause by an 'unsatisfactory' sample may help to worsen the condition and lengthen recovery.

More research by bacteriologists and nurse teams should be done to identify the most important aspects of the procedure and reduce those actions which are unnecessary or serve to mask the results. Perhaps this Manchester team will be rewarded by huge funding for same!

References

1 Macleod, J., Hockey, L. Research for Nursing. London: HM & M Publications, 1979

2 Smith, T.C.G. Specimen testing. Nursing Times 1969; 142: 19, 57-58

3 Mellings, M. Specitest for obtaining midstream specimens of urine from women. Nursing Times 1969; 65: 2, 48-49

4 Burke, C.W. Time urinary tests - the nurse's role. Nursing Times 1975; 71:46, 1813-1815

5 Stronge, J.L. Infection control audit of a nursing procedure: collection of midstream specimens of urine. Nursing Times 1976; 72: 11, 426-427

6 Werman, H.A. Utility of urine culture in the emergency department. Annals of Emergency Medicine 1986; 15: 3, 302-307

7 Marple, C. The frequency and character of urinary tract infections in an unselected group of women. Annals of Internal Medicine 1941; 14: 2220-2239

8 Beeson, P.B. The case against the catheter. American Journal of Medicine 1958; 24: 1, 1-3

9 Platt, R. Quantitative definition of bacteriuria. American Journal of Medicine 1983; xx, 44-50

10 Kass, E. H. Asymptomatic infections of the urinary tract. Transactions of the Association of American Physicians 1956; 69: 56-64

11 Stamm, W. E., Counts, G.W., Running, K. R. et al. Diagnosis of coliform infection in acutely dysuric women. New England Journal of Medicine 1982: 307, 463-467.

12 Dobbs, G. H. Bacteriuria in pregnancy, labour and puerperium. Journal of Obstetrics and Gynaecology of the British Empire 1931; 38: 773-787

13 Norden, C.W., Kass, E. H. Bacteriuria in pregnancy - a critical appraisal. Annual Review of Medicine 1968; 19: 431-470

14 Boshell, B. R., Sanford, J.P. A screening method for the evaluation of UTI in female patients without catheterisation. *Annals of Internal Medicine* 1958; 58: 5, 1040-1045

15 Polit, D.F., Hungler, B.P. *Nursing Research: Principles and Methods.*(2nd edition). Philadelphia: Lippincott, 1985.

16 Abraham, I.L., Schutz, S., Polis, N. *et al.* Research on research - the meta-analysis of nursing and health research. In: Cahoon, M.C. (ed). *Recent Advances in Nursing Research Methodology.* Edinburgh: Churchill Livingstone, 1987

17 Field, P.A., Morse, J.M. Nursing Research: *The application of qualitative approaches.* London: Croom Helm, 1985

18 Abdellah, F.G., Levine, E. *Better Patient Care Through Nursing Research.* London: Collier Macmillan, 1979.

19 *Generalised Linear Interactive Modelling* (GLIM). Release 3.77. Oxford: Numerical Algorithms Group 1986

20 Morris, R.W., Watts, M.R., Reeves, D.S. Perineal cleansing before mid stream urine collection; a necessary ritual? *The Lancet* 1979; 2: 8134, 158-159.

21 Seaman, C., Vehonick, P. *Research Methods for Undergraduate Students in Nursing.* New York: Appleton-Century-Crofts, 1982.

22 Hatcher, J. Quackery, fraud and scientific method. The history of urine testing. *Nursing Mirror* 1976; 142: 65-66.

Judith Brown wrote this while an undergraduate nursing student, University of Manchester. Joanne Meikle is a joint appointee, University of Manchester and Central Manchester Health Authority and Christine Webb is Professor of Nursing, University of Manchester.

ANSWERS TO SELF-ASSESSMENT QUESTIONS

1 No, you do not. Descriptive research questions, by definition, do not require a prediction to be made.

2 The statement 'I think that sodium intake affects blood pressure' is not a research hypothesis because:

- no variables have been specified

- there is no predicted relationship between variables

- there is no indication of measurement.

3 The null hypothesis, that the independent variable has no effect, is not accepted because there is always the possibility that the findings are not due entirely to chance. By using a more sensitive procedure, we might clearly demonstrate the effects of the independent variable.

4 When the null hypothesis, that the independent variable has no effect, is rejected, it means only that the observed differences are unlikely to have arisen by chance alone. A confounding variable could, nonetheless, be responsible for the effects observed.

5 We are using an interval scale.

6 (a) False – In interpreting the results of an experiment it is often necessary to go beyond the original research question and offer a theoretical explanation of the results.

(b) False – an experimental hypothesis may be rejected because the study did not provide a sufficiently sensitive test of the effects of the independent variable.

(c) False – if no valid inferences can be drawn from the results of an experiment then no general statements can be made.

(d) True – if an experiment lacks sensitivity then the effects of changes in the independent variable may have been obscured.

7 The title, abstract, references and appendices have still to be added.

8 Findings from other related studies can help to confirm both the internal and the external validity of an experiment which you are trying to interpret. If similar results have been obtained using different designs, procedures, analyses, participants and situations, this tends to confirm that an effect is genuine and may be generalised.

FURTHER READING

Recommended statistics books

Caulcott, E. (1992) *Statistics for Nurses*, Scutari Press.
Very thorough coverage at a fairly advanced level. Not a book to be read from cover to cover, but an extremely useful reference. Strongly recommended if you are fairly confident with numbers.

Clegg, F. (1982) *Simple Statistics*, Cambridge University Press.
This is my favourite, straightforward statistics book – good if you like cartoons and amusing examples, but could be irritating if you don't. Slanted towards psychology rather than health care.

Greene, J. (1990) *Methodology Handbook: Part 1, Correlational Research Designs and Part 2, Experimental Research Designs*, Open University.
Excellent, careful coverage of many of the important concepts. Part 2 has a wide range of statistical tests and is extremely clear and precise. This handbook was written to accompany a psychology course and is less strong on descriptive statistics.

Other further reading

Hicks, C. (1990) *Research and Statistics: A practical introduction for nurses*, Prentice Hall.
Useful discussion of the experimental approach and relevant statistical techniques.

Huff, D. (1973) *How to Lie with Statistics*, Penguin.
Not a basic stats primer, but many nice and memorable examples of what not to do.

Knapp, R. (1985) *Basic Statistics for Nurses*, Wiley.
Good clear coverage of the essentials and with a health care orientation.

Polit, D. and Hungler, B. (1989) *Essentials of Nursing Research*, Philadelphia: Lippincott.
Chapter 4 provides some useful material about theories and their role in research.

Reid, N. (1993) *Health Care Research by Degrees*, Blackwell.
This contains very clear instructions about how to use computer packages to carry out descriptive and inferential statistics.

Rowntree, D. (1981) *Statistics without Tears*, Penguin.
A useful, basic book on statistics.

REFERENCES

Baddley, A. (1982) *Your Memory: A user's guide,* Pelican.

Bagenal, F., Easton, D., Harris, E., Chilvers, C. and McElwain, J. (1990) 'Survival of patients with breast cancer attending Bristol Cancer Help Centre', *Lancet*, 336, pp. 606–610.

Bailey, K. (1987) *Methods of Social Research,* Free Press.

Berger, R. and Patchner, M. (1988) *Planning for Research,* Sage Publications.

Boore, J. (1978) *Prescription for Recovery,* Royal College of Nursing.

Brown, J., Meikle, J. and Webb, C. (1991) 'Collecting midstream specimens of urine – the research base', *Nursing Times*, 87 (13), pp. 49–52.

Burnard, P. and Morrison, P. (1990) *Nursing Research in Action*, Macmillan.

Butterworth, T. (1991) 'Generating research in mental health nursing', *International Journal of Nursing Studies,* 28, pp. 237–246.

Cassileth, B., Zupkis, R., Sutton-Smith, K. and March, V. (1980) 'Informed consent – why are its goals improperly realised?' *New England Journal of Medicine,* 302, pp. 896–900.

Caulcott, E. (1992) *Statistics for Nurses,* Scutari Press.

Clark, E. (1988) *Research Awareness: Module 9, The Experimental Perspective,* South Bank Polytechnic.

Clifford, C. and Gough, S. (1990) *Nursing Research: A skills based introduction*, Prentice Hall.

Clegg, F. (1982) *Simple Statistics,* Cambridge University Press.

Coolican, H. (1990) *Research Methods and Statistics in Psychology,* Hodder and Stoughton.

Cormack, D. (1991) 'An overview of the research process', in Cormack, D. (ed.) *The Research Process in Nursing,* Blackwell.

Couchman, W. and Dawson, J. (1990) *Nursing and Health-Care Research,* Scutari Press.

Draper, P. (1990) 'The development of theory in British nursing: current position and future prospects', *Journal of Advanced Nursing*, 15, pp. 12–15.

Gantley, M., Davies, D. and Murcott, A. (1993) 'Sudden infant death syndrome: links with infant care practices', *British Medical Journal*, 306, pp. 16–20.

Greene, J. (1990) *Methodology Handbook: Part 2, Experimental Research Designs,* Open University.

Griffiths, P. (1993) 'To believe or not to believe', *Nursing Times*, 89 (1), p. 39.

Hicks, C. (1990) *Research and Statistics: A practical introduction for nurses,* Prentice Hall.

Hicks, C. (1992) 'Research in midwifery: are midwives their own worst enemies?' *Midwifery*, 8, pp. 12–18.

Hockey, L. (1991) 'The nature and purpose of research', in Cormack, D. (ed.) *The Research Process in Nursing*, Blackwell.

Holden, J., Sagovsky, R. and Cox, J. (1989) 'Counselling in a general practice setting: controlled study of health visitor intervention in treatment of postnatal depression', *British Medical Journal*, 298, pp. 223–226.

Huff, D. (1973) *How to Lie with Statistics*, Penguin.

Knapp, R. (1985) *Basic Statistics for Nurses*, Wiley.

Ley, P. (1972) 'Primacy, rated importance and the recall of medical information', *Journal of Health and Social Behaviour*, 13, pp. 311–317.

Ley, P. (1988) *Communicating with Patients: Improving communication, satisfaction and compliance*, Croom Helm.

Ley, P. (1989) 'Improving patients' understanding, recall, satisfaction and compliance' in Broome, A. (ed.) *Health Psychology*, Chapman and Hall.

Ley, P. and Spelman, M. (1967) *Communicating with the Patient*, Staples Press.

McNeill, P. (1990) *Research Methods*, Routledge.

Moorbath, P. (1988) 'Writing references: a guide', *Senior Nurse*, 8, pp. 22–23.

Muss *et al.* (1980) reported in Ley, P. (1988) *Communicating with Patients: Improving Communication, Satisfaction and Compliance*, Croom Helm.

Nieswiadomy, R. (1987) *Foundations of Nursing Research*, Norwalk, Conneticut: Appleton and Lange.

Orem, D. (1985) *Concepts of Practice*, McGraw Hill.

Polgar, S. and Thomas, S. (1991) *Introduction to Research in the Health Sciences*, Churchill Livingstone.

Polit, D. and Hungler, B. (1989) *Essentials of Nursing Research*, Philadelphia: Lippincott.

Postman, L. and Phillips, L. (1965) 'Short-term temporal changes in free recall', *Quarterly Journal of Experimental Psychology*, 17, pp. 132–138.

Pulsford, D. (1992) 'Do we need research?' *Nursing Times*, 88 (34), pp. 42–43.

Reid, N. (1989) 'The Delphi Technique' in Ellis, R. (ed.) *Professional Competence and Quality Assurance in the Caring Professions*, Chapman and Hall.

Reid, N. (1993) *Health Care Research by Degrees*, Blackwell.

Roddham, M. (1989) *Research Awareness, Module 4: Searching the Literature*, South Bank Polytechnic.

Rowntree, D. (1981) *Statistics without Tears*, Penguin.

Sleep, J. and Grant, A. (1987) 'Pelvic floor exercises in postnatal care', *Midwifery*, 3, pp. 158–164.

Stockwell, F. (1972) *The Unpopular Patient*, Royal College of Nursing.

Todd, C., Reid, N. and Robinson, G. (1991) 'The impact of 12-hour nursing shifts', *Nursing Times*, 87 (31), pp. 47–50.

Wattley, L. and Müller, D. (1984) *Investigating Psychology: A practical approach for nursing*, Philadelphia: Lippincott.

Wilson-Barnett, J. (1991) 'The experiment: is it worthwhile?' *International Journal of Nursing Studies*, 28, pp. 77–87.

Glossary of Key Concepts

Analogue study: a term used by Ley (1988) to describe studies carried out with healthy volunteers which are intended to resemble health care situations in most relevant respects.

Bar chart: a graphical representation of data which is used when the independent variable varies in type or presence/absence.

Ceiling effect: this term is used when performance on a particular task is at a very high level. If this is the case, then improvements in performance cannot be produced by a treatment condition.

Conceptual framework: a way of viewing or classifying events or behaviour.

Debriefing: giving a full explanation of an experiment to people who have taken part.

Descriptive statistics: the two scores (one of central tendency and the other of dispersion) which are used to characterise a set of scores.

Experimental hypothesis: a prediction of a causal relationship between two or more variables which is stated in a testable form and which will be tested by carrying out an experiment.

Field experiment: an experiment which is carried out in a real-life situation.

Figure: a data summary in which a set of numbers have been converted into a graphical form.

Floor effect: this term is used when performance on a particular task is at a very low level. If this is the case, then reduction in performance cannot be produced by a treatment condition.

Horizontal axis: the line at the bottom of a graph which is used to represent the independent variable.

Inferential statistics: statistical tests which allow inferences about a population to be drawn from observations made on a sample.

Line graph: a graphical representation of data which is used when the independent variable varies in quantity or amount.

Measure of central tendency: a single score which is intended to be representative of a set of scores.

Measure of dispersion: a single score which is intended to show the spread or scatter of a set of scores.

Model: a representation, often in the form of a diagram, of some aspect of behaviour or the environment.

Null hypothesis: a statistical hypothesis which is evaluated and assessed in statistical analyses. The null hypothesis states that the independent variable exerts no effect and, therefore, that any difference between conditions in a given study has arisen by chance alone.

One-tailed hypothesis: this predicts a relationship between two (or more) variables in a particular direction.

Opportunity/convenience sample: a sample of people who fulfil particular selection criteria and are willing to take part in a study.

To pilot: materials or procedures that are piloted are tested on a relatively small sample of people to ensure that they will work efficiently in the study.

Phenomenology: this contains the essential assumption that people are active and conscious and capable of making choices about how to act.

Positivism: essentially, the assumption that, given sufficient knowledge, all aspects of the world can be explained, predicted and controlled.

Primacy effect: a term used to describe the finding that items which are presented first in a list of items tend to be recalled best.

Raw data: the actual scores that have been obtained from individuals taking part in a study.

Related: a term used to describe scores in different treatment conditions which are produced by the same or matched individuals.

To replicate: to repeat a study precisely as it is reported in a similar situation with similar participants. Replications act as a check on the reliability of the original findings.

Research hypothesis: a prediction of the relationship between two or more variables which is stated in a testable form.

Research process: the logical sequence of steps that a researcher must take when carrying out research of any kind.

Serial position curve: a graph showing correct recall of items against the serial position of items in a list.

Table: a data summary presented as a set of numbers.

Theoretical framework: a view of events provided by a theory.

Theory: a theory summarises and integrates existing knowledge, and, in doing so, suggests new predictions that can be made.

Two-tailed hypothesis: this predicts a relationship between two (or more) variables.

Unrelated: a term used to describe scores in different treatment conditions which are produced by different individuals.

Vertical axis: the line on a graph perpendicular to the horizontal axis which is used to represent the dependent variable.